BEN
HADDEN

W. H. G. KINGSTON

1st WORLD
LIBRARY
Literary Society

Ben Hadden

W. H. G. Kingston

© 1st World Library, 2008
PO Box 2211
Fairfield, IA 52556
www.1stworldlibrary.com
First Edition

LCCN: 2007935414

Softcover ISBN: 978-1-4218-9368-6
Hardcover ISBN: 978-1-4218-9468-3
eBook ISBN: 978-1-4218-9268-9

Purchase *"Ben Hadden"*
as a traditional bound book at:
www.1stWorldLibrary.com/purchase.asp?ISBN=978-1-4218-9368-6

1st World Library is a literary, educational organization
dedicated to:

- Creating a free internet library of downloadable ebooks

- Hosting writing competitions and offering book publishing
scholarships.

Interested in more 1st World Library books? contact:
literacy@1stworldlibrary.com
Check us out at: www.1stworldlibrary.com

1ˢᵗ World Library Literary Society

Giving Back to the World

"If you want to work on the core problem, it's early school literacy."

- James Barksdale, former CEO of Netscape

"No skill is more crucial to the future of a child, or to a democratic and prosperous society, than literacy."

- Los Angeles Times

"Literacy... means far more than learning how to read and write... The aim is to transmit... knowledge and promote social participation."

- UNESCO

"Literacy is not a luxury, it is a right and a responsibility. If our world is to meet the challenges of the twenty-first century we must harness the energy and creativity of all our citizens."

- President Bill Clinton

"Parents should be encouraged to read to their children, and teachers should be equipped with all available techniques for teaching literacy, so the varying needs and capacities of individual kids can be taken into account."

- Hugh Mackay

CHAPTER ONE

BEN'S HOME

On the east coast of England, there is a small hamlet surrounded by high sand-hills, with scarcely a blade of grass or even a low shrub to be seen in its neighbourhood. The only vegetable productions, indeed, which can flourish in that light soil, are the pale green rushes, whose roots serve to bind the sand together, and to prevent the high easterly winds, so constantly blowing on that coast, affecting it as much as they would otherwise do. Even in spite of the opposition of the rushes, several deserted huts have been almost entirely covered up by the drifting sand. See Note 1.

The population of the village consists of seafaring people and their families. The men form the crews of the numerous vessels employed in the herring fisheries which belong to the various fishing-places on the coast. Nowhere along the shores of England are finer sea-boats or more hardy crews to be found.

Most of the herring vessels are luggers, from thirty to forty tons burden, and entirely decked over. Each carries from eight to ten men. They are divided below into compartments, or tanks: in one compartment, salt is stowed; into another, the herrings, as soon as caught, are thrown; in a third they are salted, and are then packed away in lockers, on either side of the vessel, till she is full. She is then steered for the shore to the point nearest to a railway, or where there is a market. Each vessel has several long nets: the upper part of the net floats close to the surface of the water, buoyed up by bladders; the lower part is kept down by small bits of lead, and one end is moored to the bottom by a heavy weight. The fish, as they swim in large shoals, strike against the net as against a wall, and are caught in the meshes. Herring fishing is carried on at night, when the fish cannot see the nets. When a vessel or boat has cast out her nets, she hangs on to the lee [See note 2] end of them till the morning.

Besides these large herring luggers, many open boats are used; and great numbers of other boats from the coasts of Scotland and the North of England resort to these seas in the herring season. There is yet another class of vessels which frequent this coast. They are the deep-sea fishing smacks—cutters measuring from thirty to fifty tons, each carrying about ten men. Their nets differ much from those used by the luggers and boats. They fish with trawls, and so are called *trawlers*. A trawl is a net with a deep bag fastened to a long beam, which long beam has a three-cornered iron at each end. This beam is dragged along at the bottom of the sea, and stirs up the turbot, bream, plaice, soles, and other flat-fish which lie there; when they swim into the bag and are caught. These trawlers fish in the North Sea, sometimes a hundred and a hundred and fifty miles away from England, off the Texel. Other fishing grounds are from twelve to twenty miles off the British coast. At times, more than a hundred vessels are together, forming a large fleet. One of the oldest and wisest of the captains is chosen as their head man, and is called the admiral of the fleet.

They have, of course, many rules and laws to govern them. When they fish far from the land, they remain out six weeks,

W. H. G. Kingston

or more; and do not once, all that time, go into port. There are, however, steamers employed, which run to and fro to carry them food and fresh-water, also to take ice to them. With this ice the fish are packed, as soon as caught, in large baskets. The steamers then collect the fish from the different fishing-vessels, and carry it to London, or to the nearest port where there is a railway station. This account will give an idea of the many thousand people employed as fishermen on the eastern coasts of our country. In summer, while the weather is fine, their calling is pleasant and healthy; but when storms arise the hardships and perils are very great, and many of the men every year lose their lives, leaving widows and orphans behind them.

There was belonging to Sandhills, the little hamlet about which I have spoken, as fine and bold a set of fishermen as any to be found on the British coast. There were from fifteen to twenty families. The largest family was that of old John Hadden. He had eight sons and several daughters: three of his sons were away at sea—two of these were on board men-of-war, and the third was on board a trading-vessel; four followed his calling as fishermen, and formed part of the crew of the lugger of which he was master; the youngest, the eighth—Little Ben as he was always called, the son of his old age—was as yet too young to go regularly to sea. He, however, went with his father and brothers in the summer season, when fine weather was looked for, and he would not probably be exposed to hardships too severe for his tender years.

The fishermen of that coast were long known as rough and careless men, thinking nothing of religion, and utterly ignorant of religious truth. It used to be said of them, that as a rule they lived hard and died hard, caring for nobody, and nobody caring for them. This was too true of many, but not of all. It was not true of John Hadden. His outside was rough enough, and very much so in winter, when he had on his high fishing-boots, broad-flapped sou'-wester, thick woollen comforter, Guernsey frock, with a red flannel shirt above it, and a pea-coat over all. But he had an honest, tender, true, God-loving, and God-fearing heart. As he had been brought up, so he brought up his children in "the way they should go," trusting "that when they were old they would not depart from it."

John Hadden was able to do what many of his friends could not; he could read, having learned early in life. Not that he read very well, but well enough to study the Book of books so as to understand what it teaches. There are many, alas! who *can* read it far more easily than could John Hadden, but do *not*. How many have the Bible, but do not even look into it, treating it as though it were of less value than any common book! How many would rather read light foolish books than the "Holy Scriptures," though they "are able to make us wise unto salvation, through faith which is in Christ Jesus!"

What does that verse mean? That if we read and study the Scriptures, with faith in Christ Jesus, they will show us how we may, without fail, gain more joy, happiness, wealth, and glory than words can tell; not such as will pass away in a few short years, but such as will last for ever and ever.

John Hadden prized the Bible as the only light which could point out to him the way of eternal life. He read and read, and, more than all, he prayed as he read, till he understood the Bible well, and was able to shape his own course by it, and to point out to his sons how they might shape theirs. When he took up the Bible he humbly prayed, "Lord, teach me that I may read and understand Thy holy Word aright." These words, and the spirit of these words, he taught his children.

W. H. G. Kingston

John Hadden and his family neglected no means or opportunities of knowing more about the Bible, or of obtaining instruction. He did not say, as some do, "I can read, and I can pray; and so why should I go away from my own home and own fireside to listen to another man?" John Hadden was a real Christian, and therefore he was a humble Christian. The place of public worship was far off, and the road was rough; but John, with his wife and children, never failed when he was on shore, unless hindered by sickness, to go there on the Sunday to hear the Word of God read and explained, and to pray with other Christian people. When John and the boys were at sea, Mrs Hadden and the other children went, and she used to say she dearly loved to do so, because then she could pray with others to the good Lord, and say, "That it may please Thee to preserve all that travel by land or by water." John often also said that when he was away on the ocean, he always felt happy as the hour of public service came round, because he knew that his wife and children, and other Christian friends, would be praying for him and his companions at sea.

Among the precepts which John Hadden found in his Bible was this: "Remember that thou keep holy the Sabbath-day. Six days shalt thou labour, and do all that thou hast to do; but the seventh day is the Sabbath of the Lord thy God. In it thou shalt do no manner of work." Now John Hadden was a plain man, and he understood things plainly. When, early in life, he first understood this commandment, he determined that he would keep it; and so, while others cast out their nets on Saturday night, as usual, John always kept his in. If he could, he ran into harbour, and worshipped God with his fellow-men on shore; if not, he and his sons and the rest of his crew united in prayer: he also read to them from the Holy Scriptures, and often besides from some religious book likely to feed their souls with spiritual food. John Hadden had acted in this way for years. The masters of other boats had tried in vain to make him give up this practice. They told him he would be ruined; that he had a large family to bring up; that it was foolish, and not required; that such commandments wore for shore-going people, and not for poor fishermen. But John's answer was always the same: "I'll tell you what, mates: God says, 'Do no work on the Sabbath'—don't fish, that means; and I'm very certain that what He says is right. So it is not right to fish more than six days in the week. What I tell you, mates, and what I tell my boys, is this: '*Do right whatever comes of it.*'"

Note 1. This plant is the round-headed rush, or *Juncus conglomeratus* of naturalists, and is cultivated with great care, especially on the banks of the sea, in Holland, to prevent the water from washing away the earth; for the roots of these rushes strike very deep in the ground, and mat together near the surface so as to form a hold on the loose soil. These rushes do not grow so strong in England as in the richer soil of Holland.

Note 2. Sailors call the side on which the wind strikes, the weather or windward side, and the opposite to it the lee side. A net is cast out to windward, and the vessel drops slowly down from it till it is all out, when she remains at the lee end. Sometimes the nets are left with only a buoy to mark their position, and the vessel goes to a distance to cast out others.

CHAPTER TWO

BEN'S FATHER AND HIS MOTTO

It would be well if all, of high or low degree, landsmen and sailors, gentle and simple, kept to old John Hadden's rule. How much misery and suffering would be saved! how much remorse of conscience! how much grief and shame! How much better would Satan, that great foe of man, be kept at a distance! That is just the reason he whispers, whenever he can get an opening, "Do wrong that good may come of it," or, "Do a little wrong, just a little, and no harm will come of it;" or again, "Commit a small sin; God will not see it, or if He does, God will not care for it." That is just what Satan has been saying over and over again since he first tempted and deceived Eve in the garden of Paradise. He spoke then from envy, to drive our first parents out of an earthly paradise; he in like manner lies now to us, to hinder us from getting into the heavenly paradise, prepared for those who love and obey God. John Hadden knew this full well, and so he would allow no departure from that rule; he would have it stuck to closely. He was for ever saying to his sons, "Do right at all times, my lads; it is not your business to think of what will happen afterwards. God will take care of that; He will guide you better than you can guide yourselves. If you act as I say, no real evil will befall you. You may fancy that what happens is an evil just for the time; but, depend on it, what seems an evil will turn out for your good in the end."

A stranger, visiting in the neighbourhood, once walked over to Sandhills. He had a talk with John Hadden, who happened to be on shore. He soon found that John was a Bible-reading man, and that he obeyed the law of the gospel.

"And so you have followed this plan of yours for some time, and have found it answer?" said the stranger.

"Yes, sir," said John, "I have followed it since I was a young man, and now I am an old one. I never have fished on a Sunday, and I hope that I never shall. Look at me, sir. Am I more feeble, am I thinner, am I more sickly than my neighbours? am I less able to work?"

"No, indeed you are not," answered the stranger; "you are the stoutest and one of the most able-bodied men I have seen in the place."

"Am I poorer? is my cottage less comfortable? are my children worse educated? are they inferior in health, strength, or activity to the children of others in the hamlet?" asked John, warming with the subject.

"No, my friend," answered the stranger; "your sons are the finest young fellows in the place, and the best brought up, as I hear from all sides, while your cottage is the neatest and most comfortable."

"That it is; that's what I say to my brother fishermen," exclaimed John Hadden, warmly. "Now, sir, I will tell you more than this. Instead of being a poorer man for not fishing on a Sunday I know that I am a richer one, and I can prove it. God knows what is best for us; so in His love He gave us the Sabbath, that we might rest, and that our souls might turn to

Him and be glad. While others have been toiling all the year round, day after day, wearing out their bodies, and dulling and saddening, so to speak, their souls, I have rested one day out of seven, and on that day my strength and my spirits have been renewed. I have not grown old so fast as they have. Then again, if I had been toiling and working for the bread which perisheth, and made my sons toil and work with me, how could I have fed my soul and their souls with that bread which will make us live for ever? Instead of being steady, honest, hard-working, God-fearing young men, a credit to me, and respected by all who know them, they would have been careless, idle, and vicious. Neighbours often say to me, 'How is it, John Hadden, that your sons are good steady young men, and do as you tell them?'—then I say, 'It is just this, because I bring them up in the fear and admonition of the Lord. The Bible tells me how to bring up my children, and I do it. If you brought up your children as the Bible tells you to do, your children would make you as happy as mine do me.'

"But, sir, I was speaking about fishing on a Sunday. Now look here, sir; there is another reason why I have an advantage over those who fish every day in the week: my nets will last longer than theirs, and at the end of a couple of years are worth one-third more. While their nets have always been wet,—for they have not had time to mend them properly,—I have had mine brought on shore on Saturday morning, spread out all day in the sun, mended in the evening, and left to dry all the next day. The wear and tear of the boats and the boats' gear also have been saved. So you see that those who break God's commandments for the sake of gain do not find it all profit. There is an old saying, sir, that 'The devil's wages slip through the fingers.' Whose wages are those gained by working on the Sabbath but his? A man fancies that he has got them safe in the palm of his hand, and when he wants to spend them, they are gone. At the end of the year,—I have said it, and I know it,—by following God's commandments, simply because He has commanded, I have been a richer man than those who disobeyed them; and I know surely that I have been a stronger, a more healthy, a happier, and a more contented one.

"Again, sir, look here; many say they can't work on from the beginning to the end of the fishing season without drink: no more they can, maybe, but rest is better far than drink; and if they would take the Sabbath-day's rest they might save the cost of the week's drink, and that's more by a long way than the Sabbath-day's toil gives them. So, as I say, when we obey God we do the best thing for ourselves, even in this life; and that to my mind shows what a merciful and loving God He is. He does not want to make us suffer pain or grief, He wants to make us happy; and so all His laws are such that if we would obey them, we should be happy. It is because men do not obey them that they are unhappy. There, sir, that's my belief. I'm an old man now; but I thought so when I was a young one, and every year since I have had good cause to think the same."

"You speak nothing but the truth, my friend," observed the gentleman; "I will tell others what you have said to me, and how you have acted, and I will try to persuade them to follow your example."

"My example, sir!" said John Hadden gravely. "Say rather, sir, the same example I try to follow."

"You are right, my friend," said the gentleman, wringing the fisherman's rough hand and walking thoughtfully away.

Some time after this, John Hadden was sitting with his spy-glass resting across his knees, at the top of the highest sand-hill near the village. A strong gale from the north-east, which

W. H. G. Kingston

would not let any of the fishing-boats put to sea, was blowing. It was at the time of the year when the larger fishing-vessels are laid up. John had more than once put his glass to his eye; he now kept it there, and made a crutch of his left arm to hold it up. While thus employed, he was joined by one of his sons.

"If he don't take care he'll be on the bank as sure as my name is John Hadden," he cried out, pointing to a large ship which had stood in from the offing (that is, from the sea far off), and was trying to work to the northward. A slant of wind which would allow the stranger (see note 1) to lay well up along shore, had tempted him to stand in closer than he should have done. Old Hadden and his son watched the strange vessel for some time with great interest. Still he stood blindly on.

"There, I feared that it would be so!" exclaimed John; "and if help don't go to them before high water, not a soul of all on board will escape."

Too true: the fine ship lay fast, her broadside struck again and again by the heavy seas, which came rolling in from the eastward.

"Jem, we must go to her!" exclaimed John Hadden suddenly. "Call your brothers, lad; it won't do to let these poor fellows perish for want of help."

Scarcely two minutes passed after this, before John Hadden and his five sons—for Ben also went—were launching their yawl through the surf which broke on the sandy beach. A few of the people of the village nearest the water came running down to see the boat off, but John had not time to tell his wife and daughters of what he was going to do. He would fain have given them a parting kiss, but time was precious. He sent up a lad, though, to his home. "Tell them," he said, "we are doing our duty; we shall be cared for." Away through the foaming sea the brave men pulled their stout boat. The spray flew over her, and speedily wetted them through, but for that they cared nothing. The seas, however, sometimes broke on board, and little Ben was kept hard at work, baling out the water.

"She is well out at the end of the spit, lads," observed old Hadden; "we may get close enough for them to heave a rope on board us, if she hangs together, and I don't see that there is much doubt about her doing that."

They pulled on for some time, without any one again speaking. "She will hang very well together," observed John; "but, oh! more's the pity, they seem to be lowering one of their boats, instead of waiting for our coming, as if they could reach the shore in her." Such was indeed the case. A small boat was lowered, and several people were seen to leap into her. She shoved off, but a current, of which the strangers could not have known, swept the boat towards the breakers. In another instant she was rolled right over, and all in her must have perished. Still the Haddens, thinking that others might be left on board, pulled on lustily to give them help.

As they rowed out more to sea, they saw another boat making her way towards the wreck. She had come from a hamlet a short distance to the north of Sandhills, from which place the wreck had been seen as well as from the Haddens' village. Though she had not left the shore till after the Haddens' boat had put off, she had the wind more in her favour, so it seemed likely that she would reach the wreck as soon as they could. When more than one boat is launched to go to a wreck, there is always a rivalry among the boatmen of the coast to try who will be the first on board, and if anything had been wanting to make the young Haddens toil

W. H. G. Kingston

harder than they had been doing, this would have made them. Still, the gale blew so strong that they could scarcely make any way against the wind, and all they could do at times was to keep the boat with her head to the sea to prevent her from being swamped (or filled with water). Yet on they went. They believed that they might be able to save some of their fellow-creatures from death, and that thought was enough to make them run all risks.

The last squall had been stronger than any others. Soon after it had passed over, John Hadden took a steady look to windward. "My boys," said he, "the gale is breaking. By the time we get up to the wreck, it will be calm enough to allow us to climb on board. It is to be hoped that her crew will stick by the vessel. No! what folly! they have launched another boat, and she will meet, I fear, with the fate of the first." He was silent for some minutes, while he looked now and again towards the wreck. "I feared so!" he cried at last; "they are lost, every one of them; no man could swim through that boiling surf."

Nearly another half-hour passed after this before the two boats got up to the wreck. The gale had by this time very much abated, and, the tide having turned, the sea had gone down. The boats pulled under the lee of the wrecked vessel, which held well together, and had her crew stayed on board, they might have been saved. Not a person was to be seen on deck. The fishermen shouted loudly; no one came. It seemed certain that all must have perished. Without help from the ship it was at first difficult to get on board, except at great risk. However, after waiting some time longer, the boats were able to run alongside, and the crews reached her deck. They searched the ship through; not a human being was found on board. A fire, however, was burning in the cabin grate, and before it sat a cat, quietly licking her paws. (A fact.) Instinct had guided her better than man's sense, of which he is often so proud.

The Haddens, with the men of the other boat, began, without loss of time, to search through the ship. She was a foreigner. It was clear that those who had left her were in great fear, and had thought only of saving their lives. Many articles of value lay scattered about in the cabins. John Hadden and his sons were on deck; the rest were below.

"Hurrah!—a prize! a prize!" cried one of the men of the other boat. "A box of gold!"

"Hush!" cried one of his companions. "Don't talk of it, man. If no one else sees it, we may have it all to ourselves."

At that moment John Hadden entered the cabin. His eye fell on the box, as the men were trying to hide it; he looked at what was in it. "Friends, this property is not ours," he remarked, in a calm, firm voice; "we shall get a fair reward if we succeed in saving it. I hope, if we stay by the ship, that we may get her off, at the top of the next flood, by lightening her a little. What say you? Will you stay by my lads and me, and do the job?"

The other men, however, had set their hearts on getting the box of gold. Have it they would, and they made all sorts of excuses to get away from the ship, that they might take it with them. John Hadden was a man who not only would not do wrong himself, but would stop others, if he could, from doing it.

"Mates," he said, "I do not want to quarrel with you, or with any other men; but the goods on board this ship must remain just as we found them. I am sure that my own lads will bear me out in what I say: none of us will touch them."

W. H. G. Kingston

"Oh, we always have heard that you were a very strict man, Mr Hadden, and now we find it true enough!" replied one of the men, with a sneer.

"No," said John Hadden quietly; "I only say, 'Do right, whatever comes of it.' If we take the goods on board this ship, we should be doing wrong. And others doing so, won't make wrong right. That's all."

"Well, well; we don't want to quarrel. We wished you to share; but if you won't, you won't, and neither will get it," answered the other; "so, Mr Hadden, let's say no more about it."

John, honest and true himself, did not think that any trick was going to be played him. The other men joined him and his sons, with seeming goodwill, in getting out warps, and in heaving overboard some of the cargo. Thus they worked on till night stopped them. There was a promise of a fine night; and so, making fast their boats under the lee of the wreck, they prepared to spend the time on board till the return of day. Of course, they had to keep a watch on deck. The first watch was kept by the Haddens; the morning watch by the people of the other boat. When John Hadden and his sons awoke in the morning, and came on deck, the other boat was gone, and so was the box of gold, which had been left in the cabin.

Daylight returning, a white speck was seen away to the northward. John Hadden, as he looked through the glass, knew that it was the boat of those who had been with him. There were some sand-banks, and a narrow passage through them, by which a long distance might be saved. At certain tides this passage was dangerous, even in fine weather.

"The foolish fellows are making for the Gut!" exclaimed

John Hadden. "I would not try to go through it for any sum." Just then some clouds were seen driven across the sky by a squall; the wind struck the boat. "She's lost! she's lost!" cried John Hadden, in a tone of pity. Over went the boat; nor she, nor her crew, nor the box of gold were ever seen again.

The ship was soon got afloat, and was brought by John Hadden and his brave sons into harbour. They gained a large sum for saving the ship.

"I told you," said John to his sons, "do right, whatever comes of it. This time, much good has come to us; so it generally will. If it does not, never mind; we don't see the good—that's all. God knows best what is best. Still do right."

Note 1. When the name and character of a vessel met at sea are not known, it is spoken of by sailors as 'a stranger'; of a stranger they say *he*, but a known vessel is named *she*.

CHAPTER THREE

A SHIP IN DISTRESS

As yet the sun seemed always to have shone on little Ben. He had a good fond mother to look after him at home, and a kind father who set him a good example, taught him well, fed him well, and never took him to sea in bad weather, or let him suffer any hardships which could be helped. Seldom could a merrier, happier fellow than Ben then was be found. Dark days, however, were coming for him, of which he little thought. Thankful, indeed, should we be that our ever-kind God does not allow us to know beforehand what we may be called on to suffer.

The summer passed away, the winter returned, and the large luggers being once more laid up in harbour, John Hadden and his sons went home to spend their Christmas. It was a very happy one. Nearly all the family were together; two sons had returned from sea, a daughter had come home for a visit from service, and many a pleasant evening they spent as they sat over the cottage fire, while the sailors recounted the adventures they had met with in their voyages to distant lands. The fishermen had also their tales to tell, and many an old story was recalled to mind and recounted by John and his eldest sons, or a neighbour who had stepped in to see them. John, too, would read to his family, not only on a Sunday evening, but on every evening in the week, when he was at home, from the Book of books.

"I can't see why people should fancy, as many do, that they need read the Bible only on one day in the week. It was surely given us to be our guide not only for Sundays, but for every day. There is no business in life in which it won't tell us how to act whenever we may have any doubts about the matter," said John one evening, after he had been reading the Scriptures; and then he continued, "In every page the Bible says, 'Do right, whatever comes of it,' and that is the very thing we ought to be reminded of, day after day, for it is the very thing we are too apt to forget."

John not only read the Bible, but he profited by what he read, and so did his children; and that is the reason why they were a happy, united, and prosperous family.

Some time after Christmas, John Hadden had gone out by himself on the sea-shore, with his constant companion, his spy-glass, under his arm. He walked up and down, and his mind dwelt on many of the scenes and events of his past life; he thought of the many dangers he had gone through, and of how often he had been mercifully preserved. "People do say that the life of a fisherman is a very dangerous one," he thought to himself. "They are right. How many of those I have known have lost theirs! Not a year that I can call to mind but some friend or other has been drowned. Such may be my end. God is merciful; He knows what is best. He will not call me away, except for some good purpose."

Continuing his walk, Hadden's mind grew more and more serious, almost melancholy; yet it must not be said that his mind was one of a gloomy turn; no man was generally more cheerful. The day, however, had an effect on his spirits. The clouds gathered thickly in the sky, and hung low down; the

W. H. G. Kingston

wind moaned as it came across the dull, leaden-looking ocean, and found its way among the sand-hills, making the tall rushes bend before it. Sheets of cold mist came rolling in every now and then towards the land; and, though they swept by, they were quickly succeeded by others, till they grew denser and denser, and a regular heavy wetting mist settled down over the face of the land and the water.

John Hadden was about to turn his steps homeward, when one of his sons came to remind him that it was time to return home to tea. Just then a heavy squall burst on the land from the eastward, and the clouds and mist breaking away left a clear space all the way to the horizon.

"I'll come, Bill, I'll come, my boy," he answered, lifting, however, his glass to his eye, to take another last look over the troubled waters before he went in for the evening. Just then he caught sight of a stranger in the offing, where, outside the sand-banks, a high sea was running. He looked earnestly through his glass for half a minute.

"There is a large ship," he said to his son, "driving on towards the banks, and totally dismasted. Unless there is a pilot aboard who knows his way through the passage, he'll be on the bank to a certainty, and then, with such a night as we shall have presently, Heaven have mercy on the unfortunate people! Even if the wreck should hang together till the morning, they will be washed overboard and be lost. Though we missed saving the people from the wreck last year, through their own folly, we must not be dispirited. Perhaps we may be able to save these. Bill, go and find your brothers, and tell them that there's a ship will be on shore directly, and that we must do something to help. Say nothing, though, to your mother, boy." Bill hastened away, and old John still watched the ship.

As he had foreseen, the stranger very soon drove on to a dangerous part of the sand-banks, and the sea before long was evidently making a clean breach over the deck. In a short time all the young Haddens, and several other men, came down on the beach, bringing old John's rough-weather coat and boots, which he put on while they were getting ready to launch the boat. Little Ben came with his brothers.

Old John put his hand on the boy's shoulder, and looked earnestly into his face. "No, Ben, I'll not take thee, my child, to-day," said he; "it's over-rough work we are going on; I couldn't even tell thy mother of it; so go home, and take care of her."

Little Ben pleaded hard to be taken, but he pleaded in vain. "No, lad, no, I cannot take you," repeated the father. "Go home now, go home. It may be late before we return. Perhaps we shall be out all night, so mother will want you at home to keep her company. Read to her, lad, out of the Bible; and, I say, Ben, if thy father never comes back, remember that his last words to thee were—*Trust to God. Do right, whatever comes of it.*"

Old John Hadden then joined the young men and the rest of the boat's crew, and their united strength soon launched her, with all her gear on board, into the water; and as they all leaped in, each man seizing an oar, they quickly had her through the surf, which had begun to roll in somewhat heavily. Little Ben stood on the top of a sand-hill, and watched them as they pulled away out to sea. His eye anxiously followed the boat as she grew less and less distinct, till she was lost to sight among the breaking seas, which leaped upwards around the sand-banks. For a time he could clearly see the wreck towards which they were directing their course. Then the shades of evening increasing, and a thick mass of mist gathering round her, she also was

W. H. G. Kingston

lost to sight.

Ben, as his father had desired him, went home, and having reported that he had seen the boat get well off, sat himself down by the side of his mother, who was working with her needle before the fire, and taking the big Bible on his knees, he began to read to her out of its sacred pages. His father's mark was at the thirteenth chapter of Saint Luke's Gospel, and he read: "There were present at that season some that told Him of the Galileans, whose blood Pilate had mingled with their sacrifices. And Jesus answering said unto them, Suppose ye that these Galileans *were* sinners above all the Galileans, because they suffered such things? I tell you, Nay: but, except ye repent, ye shall all likewise perish. Or those eighteen, upon whom the tower in Siloam fell, and slew them, think ye that they were sinners above all men that dwelt in Jerusalem? I tell you, Nay: but, except ye repent, ye shall all likewise perish."

"Father was saying that to me the other day, mother," remarked little Ben. "He told me that he had known many God-fearing men to lose their lives, and many bad ones live on and remain still in their wickedness."

"Yes, my boy; God knows best when a servant of His has lived long enough. He calls us when He wants us," replied Mrs Hadden; adding, "It matters little to a Christian when or how he is taken from earth. The great thing of all is to know that we are Christians, not in name only, but in truth. And to be a Christian is to believe on and love the dear Saviour, who has done so much for us; and so to be born again of God's Holy Spirit, as the Lord Jesus Christ Himself has told us: 'For, except a man be born again, he cannot see the kingdom of God.'"

Ben read on to his mother till she told him that it was time for him to go to bed. He repeated his prayers, and then he went up and lay down in the room which he and his brothers usually occupied; but he was the only one there. Every now and then he awoke, expecting to hear them coming in; but he only heard the rain dashing against the lattice window, and the wind howling and whistling dismally. A heavy gale was blowing right on shore. Every now and then there was a flash of vivid lightning, and a loud crash of thunder rattling away across the sky. Ben tried again to go to sleep, but he could not. He was certain that his poor mother could not be sleeping. He crept down to her room, where a light was burning. Her head had not pressed her pillow; she was on her knees, with her face bent down to the bed, and her hands clasped together.

Noiselessly Ben stole back to his attic. "I can pray too, and join my prayers to mother's," he said to himself. He prayed for his father and brothers exposed in their open boat to that fierce storm near those terrific breakers, which rolled in over the sand-bank where the ship had struck. He fully understood all the dangers to which they were exposed. "God knows best what to do—God's will be done," he repeated as he rose from his knees.

Daylight came at last. Ben got up, and, slipping on his clothes, he ran out to the sand-hills, whence he could obtain a clear view over the sea. He well knew the spot where the ship had struck. She was not there, nor was there any sign of the boat. He could not bring himself to go back to his poor mother with this account, so he went down to the beach. The shore was strewed with bits of the wreck, showing the fearful character of the gale which had blown all night, and was still blowing.

Hour after hour passed by; but no boat neared the shore. His mother came to look for him, and with trembling voice

W. H. G. Kingston

called him in; yet she lingered, watching anxiously with haggard eyes the foaming ocean. At length night returned. Neighbours looked in, but they could give her no comfort. The boat might have run into port, but it was not likely. Sadly that second night passed away. The morning brought no gleam of hope. Mrs Hadden's lot has been that of many fishermen's and sailors' wives.

CHAPTER FOUR

A SORROWFUL HOME AND A NEW FRIEND

As day after day passed away, Mrs Hadden ceased to hope. Neither John Hadden nor any of his companions were ever again heard of. There could be no doubt that they had been lost in their gallant attempt to carry succour to their fellow-creatures on the wreck. Mrs Hadden was a widow and little Ben was fatherless.

"Whom the Lord loveth He chasteneth," repeated the bereaved woman over and over to herself. "Oh, may He in His mercy give me strength to bear the lot He has thought fit in His wisdom to prepare for me, and make it profitable to my soul."

She had many trials to bear. Her husband and sons, those able to support her, were gone; and some time passed before she could gather strength to arouse herself to consider what she could do for the sustenance of little Ben and herself. He was willing and eager to work, though he could not hope to gain much as yet. He soon had also another besides his mother and himself to work for. One of his sisters at service fell ill, and had to come home and be nursed; and, poor girl, it made her feel worse to know that she was thus trespassing on her mother's scanty means; though little Ben did his best

W. H. G. Kingston

to cheer her up, telling her that it was just a double pleasure to have two to work for besides himself, instead of only one.

He did his best certainly, though that was but little. His mother entreated him not to go out in the fishing-boats, for she dreaded (and that was but natural) that the same fate which had befallen his father and brothers might overtake him. He, however, bought, on credit, fish caught by others, and all the fishermen were ready to trust him. He carried them for sale to the houses of the neighbouring gentry and farmers. Sometimes, with his basket at his back, he got a lift in a cart to the nearest town, where, in the summer season, he was able to obtain a better price than he usually asked of his regular country customers. People who had once dealt with him were always ready to deal again. They found that they could without fail trust him. He could always tell the day, and almost the very hour, the fish he had to sell had been caught, and his customers found from experience that he never deceived them. At the first, when in a frank manner he told them the exact time the fish had been landed, some were inclined to laugh, and others to be angry, fancying that he was practising on their credulity; but the more generous soon saw, from the honest blush which rose on his cheeks when he assured them that he was simply saying what he knew to be the case, that he was really speaking the truth. He thus gained many friends, and even bargain-loving housekeepers ceased to try and beat him down. His price was always moderate, and the profit he made was, after all, but a small remuneration for the toil he went through.

To be up early, to be on his feet all day, and often unable to reach home till late in the evening, was now little Ben's fate. He did not complain; far from it. He rejoiced that he was thus able to assist his widowed mother.

John Hadden had saved but little money. His boat and his

nets composed the principal part of his worldly wealth, besides the cottage he lived in. The boat was gone; and the nets, without the hands which used them, could gain nothing. Mrs Hadden was therefore advised to sell them, with the portions of the boat-gear which had remained on shore. The times, however, were bad, she was told, and the things were sold very much under their real value. She was still thankful for what she received, and she resolved to live as frugally as possible, that her humble means might the longer hold out.

Her daughter was a heavy expense to her. Poor Susan grew worse and worse; yet she still lingered on, utterly helpless to look at, yet not helpless in reality, for she was supported by faith in the Lord Jesus Christ. She was perfectly happy, as far as she herself was concerned; her only regret being that she deprived her mother of part of the scanty means she so much required for herself. At length, full of hope and joy, she died. Little Ben wept bitterly for the loss of his sister: he had never for one moment thought of the money spent on her. The bereaved mother mourned more silently.

Mrs Hadden was yet to be further tried. A letter one day reached her from a stranger. It told her that her only surviving son, besides Ben, had been cast away in the far off Pacific Ocean, and, with many others, murdered or held captive by savages. The writer, Thomas Barlow, said that he and Ned were great friends, and that they had agreed, should any misfortune happen to either, the survivor should write home, and give an account of what had occurred. Barlow wrote, in fulfilment of his promise, addressing his letter to John Hadden: all the hope he could give was that Ned might have escaped with his life, as some white men had been known from time to time to be living among those savages; but the opinion was that all their shipmates had been murdered. The writer added that he, with six other men only of all the crew, had made their escape in the longboat of the

W. H. G. Kingston

wrecked vessel, and, after suffering great hardships, had been picked up at sea by a ship bound for Sydney, New South Wales.

"Poor Ned! poor Ned!" exclaimed little Ben, crying bitterly; "he must not be lost! I'll go and look for him, mother. If he is alive, I'll find him, and bring him back to you."

"Oh no! no, Ben! don't you go away from me," cried the poor widow. "I should indeed be forlorn if I was to lose you. Yet, Ned! Ned! poor Ned! where can you be—among savages, or killed? You wouldn't find him, Ben; they would only treat you in the same way, and I should lose you, Ben. It cannot be: oh, don't—don't think of it, Ben!" And the poor widow at length found some relief to her feelings in a flood of tears. It was seldom that she gave way in this manner; but the announcement of Ned's too probable fate, and the thought of losing Ben, completely overcame her.

The idea, however, that he would go to sea and find his brother had entered little Ben's head, and, moreover, that they together would bring back wealth sufficient to support their mother in comfort. That idea was not very easily driven away. Day after day it occurred to him. His difficulty was to persuade his mother to let him go. He did not understand as clearly as an older person might have done, that he could not go away without making her very unhappy. He argued that he should be away only a short time, and that then he should come back so rich, and be able to take such good care of her, that she would gain ample amends for the pain she might suffer by parting with him for a season. Poor fellow! he little knew the dangers and hardships he would have to encounter in a sailor's life.

Ben's mind was full of his plans, and they served at all events to beguile many a weary mile, as he trudged on through the country, contentedly as usual, selling his fish. One day, however, when walking along the streets of the town, he met with an accident. A horse, dragging a cart, took fright and was dashing along the road, near the sea, towards a group of little children whose nursemaids were standing chatting to each other, not thinking much about their young charges. The women, startled at hearing the horse coming, were so frightened that they knew not what to do. They snatched up one child after the other, running here and there, and leaving several of the little creatures, unconscious of their danger, in the very way of the maddened animal. Ben saw the peril in which the children were placed, and, throwing down his basket of fish, he sprang forward and caught the reins, which were hanging over the shafts. He had not strength to stop the horse, though he turned it aside, while he still hung on to the reins; he was at the same time dragged down, and the wheel passed over his side and one of his legs. The horse, thus turned from his course, dashed against some railings, and was stopped. The children were saved.

A gentleman looking out of a window saw the accident, and the gallant way in which little Ben had behaved. He rushed out of the house, took him in, placed him on a sofa, and sent for a surgeon. His leg was not broken, but some of his ribs were. The gentleman said that Ben should remain at his house till he was cured. He also at once sent off to Mrs Hadden to inform her of the accident, and to assure her that her son was well taken care of. Immediately she received the sad news, she set off to see Ben. She could not bear the thought of letting him remain with strangers, however kind they might prove.

It was almost midnight when she arrived. Ben's friend received her kindly, and her heart was comforted when she found that her son was going on so well. The gentleman told her that he was Lieutenant Charlton, of the navy, and again assured her that he would take good care of the boy. Satisfied that Ben's new friend would keep his word, she returned home the next day.

In less than six weeks Ben was almost himself again. Lieutenant Charlton nursed the poor boy as if he had been his own son, and showed how much pleased he was with him. Ben spoke frankly to him, told him of his past life, hopes, and wishes.

"Well, my boy, I will take you to sea with me when next I go, and that will be, I hope, before long," said the lieutenant to him one day.

"I should like to go, sir, very much indeed, but mother says that she cannot part with me," answered Ben.

"I will speak to your mother, and explain to her how seamen in the British navy are now treated," said the lieutenant. "She, I daresay, believes that they are no more cared for than they used to be at one time; whereas, the truth is that they are better looked after than many people on shore, and certainly much better than the seamen in the merchant service."

"It is not ill-treatment either she or I fear, sir," said Ben. "I'd go anywhere with you, sir; but mother cannot bear the thought of parting with me—that's the truth of it, sir."

"I'll speak to her about the matter, and perhaps she may see things in a different light," said Lieutenant Charlton. "Perhaps I may be able to find a home for her while you are away, and then she will be content to let you go, knowing that you are well provided for."

Ben thanked the lieutenant very much. He made up his mind, however, that, unless his mother was perfectly ready to let him go to sea, nothing should persuade him to quit her. He had not forgotten his father's last words, "Do right, whatever comes of it."

"The Bible says, 'Honour thy father and thy mother,'" said Ben to himself. "I should not be honouring my mother if I was to disobey her wishes, even though I was to become an officer, and see all the world, and come back with my pockets full of gold. No, no! Lieutenant Charlton is very kind and very good—that I am sure of; but, poor dear mother, I'll not leave her, unless she bids me, in God's name, go and prosper."

Ben was now sufficiently recovered to return home. He went back in a cart provided for him by the good lieutenant, who had also during his confinement not been unmindful of his mother. Ben found that some ladies had called on her, saying that they were the parents of the children who had been saved by Ben's bravery and presence of mind, and they insisted, as the least they could do, on supplying all her wants during his absence. They also promised further aid when they had learned how they could best bestow it. Indeed, Mrs Hadden had been much better off of late than she had been for a long time before.

"I think, mother, that we should say, besides 'Do right, whatever comes of it,' 'Whatever happens is for the best,' even though it looks to us like a great misfortune. I thought that I was very unfortunate when I got knocked down and had my ribs broken, and yet you see how much good has come out of it. You have been well looked after, and I have gained more friends than I might otherwise have found during all my life."

"Yes, Ben," answered Mrs Hadden, "yes. God orders all for the best, there's no doubt about that; but His ways are not our ways, and we cannot always see how that which happens is to work for our good as clearly as we now see how your broken ribs which you speak of have brought me many comforts I should not otherwise have enjoyed. Your father, Ben, would have said what I do; and I often think, now that he is in heaven enjoying perfect happiness, how he blesses God that he was born a poor humble fisherman, with the grace and the religious privileges he enjoyed, instead of some rich man, whose heart might have remained unchanged, or instead of one who might have put his faith in the Pope of Rome, or in that wicked impostor we were reading about, Mahomet. Ah, Ben, we often are not thankful enough for all the religious advantages we enjoy, and, above all, that we have so fully and freely the gospel placed before us."

CHAPTER FIVE

A TURN IN BEN'S HISTORY

Little Ben had now sufficiently recovered to follow his former business, for though not as strong as before his accident, he calculated on getting an occasional lift in a cart, so as to make his rounds with less difficulty. The first day he went down to the beach when the boats came in, he was welcomed with a friendly smile from all the fishermen. They had heard how he had saved the little children from being run over by the horse and cart. First one brought him a couple of fine fish, saying, "That's for you, Ben. Don't talk of payment this time." Then another did the same thing, and another, and another, till his basket was so full that he could scarcely carry it. He thanked the kind fishermen all very much, and said that he was sure he did not deserve that from them; but they replied that they were better judges than he was of that matter, and that they only wished they could afford to fill his basket in the same manner every morning. This was very pleasant to Ben's feelings, and he got so good a price for the fish, which were very fine, that he was ever afterwards able to pay ready money for all he bought.

Day after day Ben went his rounds; but, though he generally got a fair price for the fish he sold, he could scarcely gain sufficient to procure food and clothing for himself and his mother, and firing and lights, and to pay the taxes with which even they were charged. Sometimes he did not sell all the fish he had bought, and, as fish will not keep long, he and his mother had to eat them themselves, or to sell them to other poor people at a low rate. Then he wore out a good many pairs of shoes, as well as other clothes, as he had to be out in all weathers; for those who wanted a dish of fish for dinner would not have been satisfied had he waited till the next morning to bring it to them on account of a storm of rain or snow. Mrs Hadden had thought of taking to sell fish herself, to relieve Ben somewhat, but he urged her not to make the attempt. She was not strong, and, although a fisherman's wife, had been unaccustomed to out-door work. She had been in service during her younger days as a nurse, where she enjoyed every comfort she could desire. When she married, though no man's cottage was better kept than John Hadden's, and no children were better cared for and brought up, she could not help him in the way the wives of most of the fishermen were expected to do. "But then," as John remarked, when some of his friends warned him that he was a lout to marry a fine lady and a useless person, "she is a God-fearing, pious woman, and she'll do her best in whatever I wish her to do." So she did, and till the day of his death John never had reason to regret his choice.

"God will show us what ought to be done, and give the strength to do it, if I ought to go out and sell fish to obtain our daily food," said Mrs Hadden, after she had one day been talking over the subject with Ben.

"Yes, mother, there is no doubt but that God will show us what ought to be done," he answered. "But the minister was telling us on Sunday that God brings about what He wishes to take place through human means, and does not work what we call miracles; so I think that, if He hasn't given you the strength of body to carry about a basket of fish through the country, He does not wish you so to employ yourself."

The discussion was cut short by the appearance of Lieutenant Charlton, who had ridden up to the door of the cottage. Ben ran out to welcome him and to hold his horse, but he said, "No, we must get somebody else to take care of the animal while you and I have a talk with your mother over matters." Ben easily found a lad to lead his kind friend's horse up and down on the sand, and then he accompanied the lieutenant into the cottage.

"I have a great deal to say to you, Mrs Hadden, and so I hope that you will hear me patiently," said the lieutenant, sitting down in the chair John Hadden used to occupy. "First, I must tell you that I am going away to sea. I have a mother who is a great invalid, and requires the constant attendance of a sensible, good-tempered Christian woman who can read to her, and talk and amuse her. I know no person so well qualified for the post as you are. My sister, who lives with her, thinks so likewise, and will be most thankful to have your assistance. In this way, if you will accept our offer, you yourself will be well provided for. Now, with regard to little Ben. Selling fish is a very respectable occupation, but not a very profitable one, I suspect, from what I can hear, and I think that your son is fitted for something better. To be sure, he may some day become a full-grown fishmonger, but that can only be some years hence; and, from what he has told me, I find that he has a strong wish to go to sea, though, unless you were comfortably provided for, nothing would tempt him to leave you. Now you see my plan: you shall take care of my mother, and I will take care of your son. What do you say to it?"

"That I am most grateful to you for your kindness, sir," answered the widow in a trembling voice; "thus much I can say at once; but I am sure that you will excuse me for not

W. H. G. Kingston

giving a decided answer immediately. I should wish to lay the matter before God in prayer, and Ben and I will go over to-morrow morning to give you our reply, if you can kindly wait so long. I wish to do what is right; but ah, sir, it is a hard thing to have to part from my only boy, after having lost so many!"

"Though my time is short before I must join my ship, of which I am first lieutenant, and I am much hurried, I will gladly wait till to-morrow morning, that you may decide for the best," answered the lieutenant. "I shall not be, I hope, less your friend, though you may differ in opinion with me and decline my offer." The kind officer, however, before he took his departure, told Mrs Hadden, in case she should give Ben leave to accompany him, what preparations she should make for him, saying that all expenses would be borne by the friends who wished to serve her. He assured her that Ben would be well treated, and would probably find many good men on board ship, who would support him in doing right, though he would of course find many who would do their utmost to lead him astray; that, if he continued as he had begun, he would certainly be made a petty officer, and very likely, if he wished it, a warrant-officer, when he would be able to retire on a comfortable pension, and at all events, in case of being wounded, he would have Greenwich Hospital to fall back on.

Mrs Hadden and little Ben thought and talked and prayed over the subject after the lieutenant was gone, and the result was that his offer was accepted. Instead of leaping for joy, as Ben thought he should do if this conclusion were come to, he threw his arms round his mother's neck, exclaiming, "Oh, mother, mother, how can I be so cruel and hard-hearted as to think of leaving you! I'll stay with you, and work for you as before, if you wish it, indeed I will. I would rather stay—I shall be very happy at home with you."

Mrs Hadden knew that these feelings were very natural, and, believing that it was to Ben's advantage that he should go to sea with so kind an officer as Lieutenant Charlton, she would not allow her resolution to be shaken, though her mother's heart was saying all the time, "Let him give it up, and stay at home with you." Children often but little understand how much parents give up for what they, at all events, believe will benefit those children.

The lieutenant had desired Mrs Hadden to let him know as soon as she had decided, as, should Ben not go with him, he should take some other boy in his place. In spite of all she could do, tears blotted the paper as she wrote her humble thanks accepting his offer. The lieutenant remarked it, observing, "Poor woman! I suppose it must be a trial to her to part with her boy—I did not think much of that."

"Indeed it must be, my son," said Mrs Charlton, his mother, who overheard him: "I found it very hard to part with you—though I did so because I thought it was right."

"You did, mother, I am sure, and providentially I fell into good hands, and have every reason to be thankful that I went to sea," said the lieutenant.

"I trust that Mrs Hadden will hear little Ben say the same when he comes back from sea," said Mrs Charlton.

"I pray that I may be able to do my duty towards the boy, and watch carefully over him," said the lieutenant.

"Depend on it, God will aid you. He always does those who trust in Him and desire to serve Him," answered Mrs Charlton. "Tell the boy also, should he at any time appear anxious about his mother, that I also will do my best to take care of her."

W. H. G. Kingston

Mrs Hadden had indeed reason to say, "Truly God careth for the fatherless and widows who put their trust in Him."

Ben's outfitting operations now went on briskly. Some kind ladies sent a piece of strong calico to make him some shirts, and from morning to night Mrs Hadden's busy fingers were plying her needle till they were finished. Other friends supplied his different wants, and he was soon quite ready to accompany Lieutenant Charlton. The day to leave home came. The worst part of the business was parting from his mother; yet, great as was the pain, it was not so great as might have been expected. People when conscious of doing right are saved much grief and suffering; especially, if they trust in God, they know that He can and will deliver them out of all their troubles.

"I shall come back, mother, to you; I know I shall. God will take care of me; I will try and do right, and serve Him faithfully; and perhaps, mother, I may bring back Ned with me," said Ben to his mother, who had taken up her abode with Mrs Charlton. These were his last words to her as he again and again embraced her, and then, tearing himself away, he ran after the lieutenant, who was walking rapidly down the street towards the inn from which the coach started that was to convey them to Portsmouth.

Ben felt as if he had reached a new world even as he travelled along the road, much more so when he entered London itself, where Mr Charlton went to the house of a relation. Ben was shown into the kitchen, and handed over to the care of the page. He found that, at the very outset of his career, he was to meet with temptation to do wrong. After the late dinner, the page came down with two rich-looking dishes untouched, and took them into a little room, where he had invited Ben to meet him.

"Be quick, let us eat them up," he said, "all but a small part of each; the housekeeper will never find it out, and I can tell cook how much I heard people praising them."

"No; unless the housekeeper or cook gives it to us, I will touch nothing," answered Ben stoutly.

"Nonsense! wherever did you learn such stuff?" exclaimed the page in surprise. "Why, we think nothing of that sort of thing; what harm can come of it?"

"I don't see that that has anything to do with the matter," said Ben. "I've been taught always to do right, whatever comes of it; and 'tis doing very far from right to take what doesn't belong to one; it is doing very wrong—it is stealing."

"I never should have thought that," said the page; "I wouldn't steal sixpence from no one, that I wouldn't! but just taking something out of a dish of good things that comes down from the parlour is altogether different."

"Now I don't see any difference at all," said Ben, more earnestly than before; "the long and the short of the matter is, that it's wrong, and we mustn't do wrong even if we fancy good is to come out of it. Just the contrary: we must do right, whatever we think may come out of it. God says, '*Do right.*' He'll take care of the rest."

The page did not utter another word, and Ben had the satisfaction of seeing him take the dishes into the housekeeper's room. This was a great encouragement to him. "If I can persuade one person to do right in what he thinks a trifle, I may persuade others; and, at all events, I will go on, with God's help, doing so whenever I have an opportunity," said Ben to himself. "That is right, I know."

The page was not at all the less friendly after this, but he treated Ben with much more respect, and Ben was very sorry to part with him. Nearly his last words to him were, "Never mind what you have been accustomed to think or to do, but just remember to do right at all times. Jesus Christ, who came on earth to save us, and to teach us how to live and act in the world, has left us an example that we should walk in His steps. And if we were always to ask ourselves what He would have done if He had been put in our place, and do accordingly, that will be the right thing for us."

Ben spoke so naturally and so earnestly, that the page didn't think it anything like canting; but he answered, "I'll try and do what you say, Ben, and when you're away at sea perhaps you'll remember me, and ask God to show me what's right. He's more likely to listen to you than to me."

"Oh no, no! don't suppose that for a moment!" exclaimed Ben. "He's ready to hear all who call upon Him faithfully. He's very kind, and loving, and gentle. He waits to be gracious. We should never get better if we waited to get better of ourselves. We must go to Him just as we are, trusting in the Lord Jesus Christ to wash away our sins; that will do it—nothing else."

Little Ben had an advantage over a very large number of people, educated and rich, as well as poor and humble. He had been all his life accustomed to read the Bible, and so he knew more about God and His will, and could talk more rightly about Him, than those who do not read God's Word can possibly do. He went daily to the fountain, and kept his pitcher full of the water of life. They who seldom or never go, must have their pitchers empty.

CHAPTER SIX

LIFE ON SHIPBOARD

Mr Charlton had been appointed as first lieutenant of the Ajax, a thirty-six gun frigate, fitting-out for the Pacific station. On his arrival at Portsmouth, he at once repaired on board, taking Ben with him. As they pulled up the harbour in a shore boat towards the frigate, which lay lashed alongside a hulk, Ben was astonished at the number of ships he saw, and the vast size of many of them. It seemed to him as if the wind could never affect such monstrous constructions, even to move them along through the water; and as to the sea tossing them about as it did the boats to which he was accustomed, that seemed impossible. Several of them carried a hundred huge iron guns, and others even a larger number. He saw many more on the stocks in the dockyard, and others moored up the harbour, and he thought to himself, "Now, if people of different nations would but live at peace with each other, and try to do each other all the good in the world they can, instead of as much harm as possible, and employ their time in building merchant vessels and other works for the advantage of their fellow-creatures, how very much better it would be!"—Many wise and good men think as did little Ben, and yet they have to acknowledge that, while nations continue wickedly ambitious, and jealous of each other's wealth and power, it is the duty of governments to be armed

W. H. G. Kingston

and prepared to resist aggression.

Ben felt very much astonished, and almost frightened, when he found himself on board the frigate, at the din and bustle which was going forward, and the seeming confusion—the shrill whistle of the boatswain, and the hoarse shouting of his mates, as yards were swayed up, and coils of rope and stores of all sorts were hoisted on board. Ben could not understand one-half that he heard, so many strange expressions were used—indeed, there seemed to be a complete Babel of tongues, with, unhappily, much swearing and abuse. Ben thought that the work would have gone on much more satisfactorily without it. He observed, after a time, that which appeared confusion was in reality order. Each gang of men was working under a petty officer, who received his orders from superior officers, of whom there were three or four stationed in different parts of the ship; and they, again, were all under the command of the officer in charge. Each man attended only to his own business, and, let all the petty officers bawl as loud as they might, he was deaf to the voice of every one of them except to that of the officer placed over him. As Ben was left standing by himself alone, he had an opportunity of making observations on what was going forward. He would have naturally formed a very unfavourable opinion of a man-of-war, had he seen her only thus in all the hurry of fitting-out. He was beginning to think that he was forgotten, when a boy of about his own age, neatly dressed in white trousers, and shirt with a broad worked collar, came up to him, and said—

"The first lieutenant wants you: come with me."

Ben was very glad to move.

"What's your name?" asked the boy.

Ben told him.

"Mine is Tom Martin," said his companion; "I'm the boatswain's son. Mr Charlton says I'm to look after you, and tell you what you want to know. But you've been to sea before, haven't you?"

"Only in fishing-boats," answered Ben; "and I shall be much obliged to you for telling me what I ought to know."

"As to that, you'll soon pick it up; for you don't look like one of those chaps who come aboard with the hay-seed still in their hair," said Tom. "Here we are at the gun-room door."

Mr Charlton's voice and eye were as kind as ever, though he spoke in rather a stiffer manner than was his custom on shore. He told Ben that he had had his name entered on the ship's books, and that the boatswain would look after him, and give him instruction with his own son; besides this, that he was to be one of the boys employed in attending on the gun-room officers, which was an advantage, as it would give him plenty to do, and some little pay besides.

"You may go forward now," said Mr Charlton. "The gun-room steward will tell you what to do when he comes on board. And remember, Martin, I shall depend on you to show Hadden everything he ought to know, and all about the ship."

"Ay, ay, sir," said Tom, pulling a lock of his hair, as of course he held his hat in his hand. Then he gave Ben a nudge, to signify that he was to come away with him.

"You are a lucky chap to have the first lieutenant for your friend," observed Tom, as they went forward.

"Yes, he's a kind, good gentleman as ever lived," answered

Ben warmly.

"That may be; but what I mean is, if you keep wide awake, and try to win his favour, you'll have a comfortable time of it, and get a good rating before the ship is paid off," observed Tom.

Ben, resolved as he was to keep to his principles, and to be ready to own them on all fit occasions, looked at his companion, and said, "I know, Martin, there's one thing I have to do, and that is, to do right whatever comes of it. If I do right, I need have no fear but that, in the long-run, I shall please the first lieutenant and all the officers; at any rate, I shall please God, and that's of more consequence than anything else."

"Oh, I see what sort of a chap you are!" observed Tom. "Well, don't go and talk like that to others—they mayn't take it as I do; for my part, I don't mind it." And Tom put on a very self-pleased, patronising air.

"I don't see that I have said anything out of the way," remarked Ben. "It stands to reason that to do right is the only way to please God, and that to please God is the wisest thing to do, as He gives us everything we have; and of course He will give more to those who try to please Him than to those who do not. There are many other reasons, but that is one, is it not?"

"Yes, I suppose so; but I haven't thought much about such things," said Tom.

"Then do think about them. I know that it is a good thing to do," said Ben.

"I'll try," whispered Tom.

It must not be supposed that Ben and Tom often talked together like this at first. There was too much bustle going forward for anything of the sort; they, as well as everybody in the ship, were kept hard at work from sunrise to sunset, and they were both so sleepy at night, when they turned into their hammocks, that they instantly fell fast asleep.

Ben had thus an opportunity of observing the whole process of fitting-out a ship. First he saw the huge, heavy guns hoisted on board, by means of tackles, with as much ease as an angler draws a big fish out of the water; then they were mounted on their carriages, and secured along the sides. Tackles, he learned, are formed by reeving ropes several times backwards and forwards through blocks. Then the topmasts and yards were got on board, swayed up, and crossed. Next, stores of all sorts were brought alongside—anchors, and chain-cables, and coils of rope, and round shot, and sails, and canvas, and paint, and tools for the various departments, and muskets, and cutlasses, and pistols, and bullets. No powder, however, came; and Ben learned that that would not be brought on board till the ship was out at Spithead. This rule was made because of accidents which had occurred formerly, ships having been blown up in the harbour, and been not only themselves destroyed, but caused the destruction of others, and the lives of very many people. Ben, however, saw the place where it was to be kept—a room lined with iron, with two doors. Between the doors was a sort of anteroom, and the outer door had an iron grating in it. There were means of flooding the magazine, in case of the ship catching fire. Last of all, the provisions and water were got on board—casks of beef and pork, and flour, and groceries, and spirits; and there were candles, and clothing, and (more necessary than most other things) water came alongside in lighters, and was pumped up into large iron tanks at the bottom of the ship. These tanks were large enough to allow a person to get into them to clean them out.

W. H. G. Kingston

They were in the inside coated with lime, and Ben was told that the water was kept in them fresh and pure for years.

The tools and stores were under the charge of three different warrant-officers—the gunner, the boatswain, and the carpenter. The first had everything connected with the guns, the shot, and powder; the boatswain had charge of all the ropes, sails, anchors, and cables; and the last of all, the woodwork, and spars, and pumps.

The provisions and clothing were under charge of the purser, who was an officer of superior rank, living with the lieutenants and surgeon. There was another officer, called the master, who also ranked with the lieutenants. He had charge of the navigation of the ship.

When the ship was completely fitted out, a body of soldiers called marines, under the command of a lieutenant, came on board. There was also one cabin full of young gentlemen, called midshipmen, their ages varying from thirteen up to five or six-and-twenty; with them, however, were the captain's and purser's clerks, and master's assistants, and assistant surgeons. They had two or three boys to attend on them. Ben was very glad that he was not selected for the duty, as the young gentlemen were frequently somewhat thoughtless in the way they treated the boys.

Above all the rest was the captain, who was answerable to no one on board; but he was bound by certain laws laid down for his guidance, and, if he broke any of them, would have to explain the reason to the Government at home, administered by the Board of Admiralty.

Ben soon understood that all these people could not live together in harmony, nor the ship be properly managed, without prompt and exact obedience to all laws and orders.

The captain must obey the laws—the articles of war, as they are called—and the rules and regulations of the service, and all the officers and men the orders issued by those above them.

One of the last things done was to bend the sails, that is, to stretch them out on the yards; and the men were then exercised in furling them, which means, rolling them up; in again loosing them; and in reefing, that is, reducing their size by rolling up only a portion of each sail. At length, the ship being ready for sea, she sailed out to Spithead. As Ben, who was on the forecastle with Tom Martin, saw her gliding through the water for the first time, like a stately swan, he felt very proud of belonging to her, though he was nearly the youngest boy on board, and of the least consequence. "So I am," he said to himself, recollecting this; "but still, though I am but small, I can do as well as I am able whatever I am set to do; that, at all events, will be doing right." Ben thought rightly that no one is too young or too insignificant to do his best in whatever he is set to do, never mind what that doing may be.

The powder was received on board, and until it was stowed carefully away in the magazine, all lights were extinguished. If people were as careful to avoid sin and its consequences as sailors are to avoid blowing up their ship, how different would be the world from what it is! Yet how far more sad are the consequences of sin!

A few more stores and provisions came off; so did the captain. Blue Peter was hoisted [see note 1]; all visitors were ordered out of the ship; despatches and letters for many distant places she was expected to visit were received; the anchor was hove up to the merry sound of the fife as the seamen tramped round and round the capstan, and, her canvas being spread to the wind, she glided majestically

W. H. G. Kingston

onward, her voyage now fairly commenced.

The wind was fair, and the frigate quickly ran down Channel, and took her departure from the Lizard, one of the south-western points of England. She had a wide extent of ocean before her to traverse, and many weeks would pass before land would be again sighted. Still, the master, with the aid of the compass, his sextant, and chronometer, was able to steer his course with as much certainty as if land had been all the time in sight.

Martin told Ben, jokingly, that the object of the sextant was to shoot the stars and the sun; but Ben found that it was to measure the height of the sun above the horizon, and the distance of certain stars from each other. The chronometer, he learned, was a large watch made to keep exact time, so that the time in London was known wherever the ship went. Ben saw another instrument, a reel with a long line and a triangular piece of board at the end of it. The line was divided into twelve or more parts; the end with the board attached was thrown overboard, and, as the line ran out, a seaman held up a little sand-glass shaped like an hour-glass. By it the number of knots or divisions run out were easily measured, and the number of miles the ship sailed over in one hour was ascertained, and the distance made good each day calculated. Ben looked at the compass with the greatest respect, and was much pleased when Mr Martin, the boatswain, could take him and Tom aft to explain its use to them, and to show them how the ship was steered. As they were not officers, they could not go when they liked to that part of the ship, only when they were sent to perform some piece of duty.

Ben seldom exchanged a word with Mr Charlton, who, however, never failed when he passed to give him a kind glance of the eye, to show him that he was not forgotten.

This made him feel happy and contented. People of all ages feel thus when they know that a kind friend is looking after them. How much more, then, should Christians feel happy and contented when they know that their Father in heaven, the kindest of friends, and at the same time the most powerful, who never slumbers nor sleeps, is ever watching over them to guard them from all evil; and that if He allows what the world calls a misfortune to overtake them, it is for their real good.

Ben soon learned all about a ship, for, having been from his childhood on the water, things were not so strange to him as they are to a boy who had come from some inland place with, as Tom said, the hay-seed in his hair. He was as active and intelligent and daring as any of the boys in the ship, not only of his own size, but of those much bigger and older. Though also he had his duties in the gun-room to attend to, he learned to go aloft, and to furl and reef sails, and to knot and splice, and to perform many other tasks required of sailors. He made many friends, too, among the best men and the petty officers, for he was always obliging and ready to serve any one he could in a lawful way; but any one who had asked Ben to do what he knew to be wrong would have found him very far from obliging.

Day after day the frigate sailed on over a smooth ocean, it being scarcely necessary to alter a sail, but the crew were not idle; the ship had to be got into perfect order below, and there was much painting, and cleaning, and scrubbing; then the men were exercised in reefing and furling sails, and going through all the operations necessary to bring the ship to an anchor. Though no gale threatened, topgallant masts and their yards were sent down on deck, and everything was made snug, so that they might quickly make the proper preparations when one should come on. The men were also daily exercised at the guns. To each gun a particular crew was attached, who cast it loose, went through all the movements of loading and firing over and over again, and then once more secured it. Sometimes powder was fired, and, whenever there was a calm, an empty cask with a target on it was towed off some way from the ship, and shot were fired at it.

On several occasions, in the middle of the night perhaps, that dreadful sound of the fire-bell was heard, and then the men sprang into their clothes—each man going to his proper station; the fire-buckets were filled, the pumps manned, and all stood ready to obey the orders of their officers to meet the danger. "Very well, my men; you were quickly at your stations," cried the captain. "Pipe down." The men then returned to their hammocks. Really there was no fire, but they were summoned to their posts that, in case a fire should take place, they might be cool and collected, and know exactly what to do. This was very different from "calling wolf," because a sailor *must* obey whatever signal is made to him or order given by his superior, without stopping to consider why it is issued. When the drum beats to quarters, he must fly to his station, though he knows perfectly well that no enemy is near.

One day Ben and Tom, with the gunner, the purser's steward, and the sergeant of marines, were seated in the boatswain's cabin to enjoy what he called a little social and religious conversation. All the party were above the average in intelligence. This was shown by their having risen from their original position. Various subjects had been discussed.

"To my mind, as I have often said, a ship is just like a little world," observed Mr Martin, who had some clear notions on many matters. "Every man in it has his duty to do, and if he doesn't do it, not only he, but others, suffer. It is not his business to be saying, Why am I to do this? Why am I to do that? It's the law in the articles of war, or the rules and regulations of the service; that's enough. If you join the service, you must obey those rules. It's your business, though, to learn what they are. Now, that's just the same when a man becomes a Christian. He mustn't do what he would like to do according to the natural man; but he must learn Christ's laws, and try and obey them. Just see how the men on board a man-of-war are practised and exercised in all sorts of ways to make them good seamen. Here they are, from morning till night, exercising at the guns, shortening sail, reefing topsails, drilling with the small-arms, mustering at divisions, going to quarters, and fifty other things; and though sometimes they don't like the work, it's all for their good and the good of the service, and to enable them to support the honour and glory of our country. Just in the same way, I've often thought, God manages us human creatures. We are sent into the world to fit us to become His subjects; we are exercised and practised in all sorts of ways, and, though we often think the way very hard, we may be sure that it is for our good, and, what is more, to fit us to support His honour and glory."

"I never saw the matter in that light before," observed Mr Thomson, the gunner. "I've often thought how there came to be so much pain and sorrow in the world, and how so many things go wrong in it."

"Why, look ye here, Thomson, just for this cause, because men don't obey God's laws," exclaimed Mr Martin. "Adam and Eve broke them first, and their children have been breaking them ever since. Sin did it all. What would become of us aboard here, if the ship, however well-built she might be, was badly fitted out at first, and if we all were constantly neglecting our duty and disobeying orders? Why, we should pretty soon run her ashore, or founder, or blow her up, or, if we met an enemy, have to haul down our flag."

The sergeant and purser's steward, who were both serious-minded men, though not much enlightened, agreed heartily with Mr Martin; and Ben learned many an important lesson from listening from time to time to their conversation.

Their example had also a very good effect on the ship's company generally; there was far less swearing and quarrelling and bad conversation than in many ships; for even the best of men-of-war are very far from what they should be. In course of time three or four of the men met together regularly for prayer, reading the Scriptures, and mutual instruction; and by degrees others joined them. As they were very anxious to have a place where they could meet free from interruption, Mr Martin allowed them the use of his storeroom, which, though the spot was dark and close, they considered a great privilege. He also occasionally united with them, and came oftener and oftener, until he always was present unless prevented by his duty. Ben gladly accompanied him, and he also took Tom with him; who, however, did not appear to value the advantage, for he was generally found fast asleep in a corner at the end of the meeting.

Altogether the Ajax was a happy ship. On one important point the widow's prayers for her son were heard, and Ben was kept out of the temptations and the influence of bad example to which poor sailor boys are so often exposed.

Note 1. A blue flag so called; it gives notice that the ship is about to sail.

CHAPTER SEVEN

AMONG THE ICEBERGS

Ben found the weather growing hotter and hotter as the ship approached the line, which Mr Martin told him was not really a line, but only a circle supposed to be drawn round the widest part of the globe, and where the sun at noon appears directly overhead. Still no one was much the worse for the heat; and gradually, as the ship sailed farther south, the weather became cooler and cooler, till it was as cold as it is in the winter in England; and Ben learned that the frigate was approaching the southern pole. She was then to sail round—not the pole, but a vast headland called Cape Horn; and on the other side, that is to say, to the west of it, to enter the wide Pacific Ocean. Ben had shown so much intelligence, and had made himself so generally useful, that Mr Charlton had placed him in a watch, that he might learn to do his duty by night as well as by day.

Scarcely had the ship's head been turned to the west than heavy weather came on. The seas rolled in vast watery heights one after the other in quick succession, so that no sooner had the frigate risen to the foaming summit of one high wave, than she sank down into the other, surrounded by dark, watery precipices, which looked as if they must break on board and overwhelm her. Ben, as he stood on the deck of

W. H. G. Kingston

the big ship of which he had become so proud, and watched the succession of the mountainous seas on every side, felt how insignificant she was, how helpless were all on board, unless trusting in the protection of God. Now she would slowly climb up the top of a huge sea; there she would remain, other seas following and seeming to chase the one on which she rode; then down again she would glide into the valley, once more to rise to the crest of another sea. If the spectacle was grand and awful in the daytime, much more so was it at night, when the ship went rushing on into darkness, no one knowing what she was to encounter ahead. The danger was not only imaginary, but real, for she was already in the latitude of icebergs, which, at that season of the year, float far away north from their original positions.

The captain had charged all on deck to keep a very sharp look-out, and Mr Charlton had said to Ben, "You have as bright a pair of eyes as anybody on board. Keep them wide open, and if you see anything like a glimmer of light through the darkness, and feel the cold greater than before, sing out sharply, there will be an iceberg ahead."

Ben resolved to do as he was told, but he did not think it likely that a little fellow like himself could be of much use. He would naturally have been very much alarmed had he been by himself in such a position, but he saw every one round him cool and collected, and he therefore felt free from fear. The four hours of his watch had nearly expired. He had been all the time peering into the darkness, thinking more than once that he saw what he had been told to look out for. Mr Martin and three or four of the best men in the ship were on the forecastle with him, all likewise looking out. Suddenly he saw what appeared like a huge sheet shaken before him by invisible hands, and a chill struck his cheek. This was what he was to look for. He sang out lustily, "An iceberg ahead—right ahead!"

"Starboard the helm!" sang out a voice from aft; and at those words the sheets and traces were flattened aft, while every man on deck flew to his post. In another instant the stout ship would have been a helpless wreck, foundering under the base of a huge iceberg. There was no space to spare. Foaming, roaring seas were seen dashing against its sides as the toiling frigate ploughed her way past it, near enough, Mr Martin said, to heave a biscuit on it. Some minutes passed before any one breathed freely; the danger had been so great and terrible that it was difficult to believe that it had passed away.

"You deserve well of us, Ben; and, depend on it, the captain and Mr Charlton are not likely to overlook what you have done," said Mr Martin. "Though I had my eyes wide open, I did not see the berg till some seconds after you had sung out; and in a touch-and-go matter, a few seconds makes all the difference whether a ship is saved or lost."

There was great danger as the ship sailed on, with the seas on her side, of their breaking on board, and she was therefore once more kept away before the wind. The watch was called, and Ben turned in. All those now on deck kept their eyes very wide open, watching for another iceberg, which it was likely they might meet with. Ben in his hammock slept soundly; he had prayed, and commended himself and all with him to his heavenly Father's protection. "If the ship should sink, I may awake and find myself with Him; but why should I fear? He will, I know, receive me graciously, and I shall meet my dear father and brothers with Him." And with such thoughts the Christian sailor boy dropped asleep.

For several days the ship ran on, the captain hauling up gradually to the north as the weather moderated. Her course was then somewhat easterly, and after some time a report ran through the ship that land might any hour be seen on the starboard bow; that is to say, on the right side. It was said that, on such occasions, the person who first discovered land often received the reward of a sovereign, or half a sovereign; and when Ben heard this, he became very anxious to obtain it. He had been the first to see the iceberg, why should he not be the first to see land? He was afraid, however, that his chance was small, as he had his duties in the gun-room to attend to, and he could seldom get away long enough at a time to go to the masthead. Still he determined to try. One thing struck him as very wonderful, that, after sailing on so many weeks, and not having once seen land, the officer should be able to tell the exact spot at which they should arrive, and the time within a few hours.

The place for which the frigate was bound is called Valparaiso, in the republic of Chili. She was, after leaving it, to go in search of the admiral on the station, and then to proceed on her voyage across the Pacific Ocean. Mr Martin told Ben and Tom that the Pacific is full of groups of islands, some of them of considerable size, with lofty mountains on them; others composed of coral, many of them measuring not a mile from one end to the other, and raised but a few feet above the surface of the ocean.

"Ah, among so many, what chance shall I have of finding Ned?" sighed Ben.

"Why, as to chance, my boy, about as much chance as finding a needle in a bundle of hay," answered Mr Martin. "But I thought, Ben, you knew better than to talk of chance. If your brother is alive,—and you shouldn't count too much upon that,—if it's God's will that you should find him, you will; but, if not, though we should visit fifty islands,—and I daresay we shall see more than that number,—you won't."

"I know, I know. I don't mean chance. Not a sparrow falls to the ground but God sees it; but I mean that, among so many islands, it is less likely that the frigate should visit the one where Ned may be."

"As I said before, if God means you to find your brother, even though there were ten times as many islands as there are, and the ship was only to visit twenty of them, or ten, or five of them, or only one for that matter, you will find him. All you have to do is to trust in God that He'll do what is best."

"Yes, I know that," said Ben. "Father always used to say, 'Do right, whatever comes of it.' God will take care that good will come out of it in the end."

　　　　　　W. H. G. Kingston

CHAPTER EIGHT

DO RIGHT, WHATEVER COMES OF IT

"Land! land!" shouted little Ben, from the foretop-masthead; for he had been out of his hammock and aloft before break of day, that he might have the best opportunity of seeing land if it was to be seen. "Yes, yes, that must be the land; those are tops of mountains covered with snow, just what Mr Martin told me might be seen before sunrise. Land! land! away on the starboard bow!" he shouted more loudly.

The officer of the watch heard him, and was soon, with his telescope slung over his shoulder, ascending the rigging. Ben pointed out the direction in which he saw the snow-capped peaks.

"You have a sharp pair of eyes, boy Hadden," observed the officer, who was looking through his glass; "those are the Andes or Cordilleras, sure enough, though seventy miles off at least—it may be many more than that."

Ben thought that he must indeed have a sharp pair of eyes, if he could see an object seventy miles off; yet he found that the officer was correct. All the men aloft now saw the mountains, and very soon they could be perceived by those on deck. Shortly after the sun rose, however, thin and light mists ascended, and veiled them from view. Still the ship sailed on with a fair breeze, hour after hour, and no land appeared. Ben began to fancy that he must have been mistaken. He was somewhat surprised, therefore, when he was sent for into the captain's cabin.

"I find that you were the first to see land this morning, boy Hadden," said the captain in a kind tone. "There is no great merit in that, but after a long passage it might be of much consequence, and I wish to reward you. You, however, rendered me a far greater service when you discovered the iceberg rounding Cape Horn. I shall not forget that. In the meantime I present you with a sovereign, to show you that I approve of your conduct on that and other occasions."

Ben, thanking the captain, left the cabin, highly pleased at the praise he had received, and very glad also to get the sovereign; not that he might spend it on himself, but that he might send it home to his mother; and he had some notion that he could do so by some means or other, but how, he could not tell. He would consult Mr Martin.

"Oh, it was to get that gold sovereign which made you so eager about going aloft of late," observed Tom, who was somewhat jealous of his companion.

"Yes. I wanted it to send to my mother," answered Ben quietly.

"But she can't want it. I never send my mother anything, nor does father, that I know of," exclaimed Tom. "Much better, Ben, to spend it like a man ashore. We could have rare fun with it, depend on that."

"My mother is a widow, and that is one reason why she should want the money, though yours doesn't," said Ben.

W. H. G. Kingston

"Then, though I came to sea in the hope of finding Ned, I also came that I might get money to take care of mother in her old age; so I think it right to send her the first sovereign I have got, and I hope that it will be followed by many more."

"You are always talking about doing right in this thing and that; but how do you know what is right?" exclaimed Tom, vexed at the idea that he should not benefit, as he thought he ought to do, by the gift his messmate had received.

"How can you ask that?" said Ben. "Haven't we got the Bible to show us in the first place, and if we can't make up our minds clearly on the matter from it, which, I allow, is possible, then cannot we pray to be guided aright? and does not God promise that He will hear our prayers, and send the Holy Spirit to guide us?"

"Yes, I know all that," answered Tom, turning away. In truth, Tom ought to have known it as well as Ben, for his father had frequently told him the same; but, though he had heard, the words had passed from one ear out at the other: he had not taken them in.

Early in the day the master had stated the hour at which the coast-line of South America would be seen; for the mountains Ben had discovered are several miles inland, and are many thousand feet high—indeed, the range of the Andes is one of the highest in the world. It now appeared at the hour the master said it would, standing up rocky and broken, from the very margin of the ocean. As the frigate drew nearer, the land looked very dry and barren, and utterly unworthy of the name it bears.

"If you were to see it in winter, just after the rains are over, you would speak very differently of it," observed Mr Martin, who had been there before. "Never judge of things, and, above all, of countries, at first sight. At the right time this country looks as green and fresh and beautiful a country as you need ever wish to see."

In the afternoon the frigate anchored in the bay of Valparaiso, which is lined by lofty hills, underneath one of which, and climbing up the sides, the town is built.

Ben was very anxious to go on shore, that he might inquire among all the sailors he could meet if any of them had heard anything of his brother Ned. Mr Charlton knew this, and arranged that he might have the opportunity of carrying out his plans as far as possible. Whenever a boat left for the shore, Ben was therefore allowed to go in her. Soon after their arrival, a boat in which Ben went was sent from the frigate under command of a midshipman, who had some commission to perform in the town. On leaving the boat, the midshipman said, "Two of you will remain as boat-keepers; the rest may step on shore, but are not to stray out of sight of the boat. Remember, these are the captain's orders."

"Ay, ay, sir," was the answer; but no sooner had the midshipman disappeared up the street, than the men all jumped on shore to look out for a grog-shop. Not one was to be seen, and on that account the place had been selected by the captain for the landing of the boat's crew. In vain they searched.

"Now, Ben Hadden, here's a job for you," said the coxswain of the boat, when they had come back and sat down in rather a sulky mood. "Just you scud up the street, and bring us down a couple of bottles of arguardiente. You are certain to find some place where they sell it, and there's five shillings for yourself. I know you want money to send to your mother; Tom told me so. Very right in you. Come, be sharp about it, there's a good lad."

W. H. G. Kingston

"Thank you, Brown," said Ben, not moving from his seat; "but you forget that Mr Manners said it was the captain's orders no one should go out of sight of the boat. Even if you were to offer me five pounds for mother, I couldn't go—"

"Oh, nonsense, boy!" answered Brown; "it isn't the money you care about, I know, but do it just to oblige us."

"No, no, Brown. I have been taught always to do right, whatever comes of it, and never to do wrong, even if it seems as if no harm would come of it," said Ben firmly.

"All right, I daresay, boy; but surely there's no harm in getting some grog in this hot weather," argued Brown.

"It's against orders, it's against the regulations, it's disobedience," returned Ben. "We were ordered not to go out of sight of the boat, and unless we do the arguardiente cannot be got."

"Oh, this is all shilly-shallying humbug!" exclaimed Brown angrily. "Come, a couple of you, with me, and we'll have the liquor, and be back in a jiffy."

"Remember, Brown, if you do, and I am asked, I'll speak the truth, I'll warn you," said Ben undauntedly.

"And I'll break your head, if you do!" exclaimed Brown, springing out of the boat, followed by two of the other men, while the rest soon scattered themselves about the quay, leaving Ben sitting in the boat. He, at all events, determined not to move, though the proper boat-keepers deserted their post. He sat on for some time, watching people passing on shore: blacks, and brown men, the aboriginal natives of the country, and white people descended from Spaniards, in their varied and picturesque costumes; and two or three processions passed, of priests, in white and purple dresses, and some in gold and scarlet, with banners of the Virgin Mary and saints, and crucifixes, and images, and bells tinkling, and men and boys chanting and swinging about incense, just as Ben had read used to be done in heathen days, but quite different to the custom of Protestant England. Some of the priests were going to visit the sick and dying, and others were on their way to attend funerals; indeed, there seemed to be a good deal of commotion on shore among the ecclesiastics. Ben could not, however, exactly tell what it all meant.

A considerable time thus passed, and he wished that his shipmates would return to the boat, lest Mr Manners should come down before them. The boat had begun to move about a good deal lately, and Ben, on looking round, discovered that a heavy sea was rolling into the harbour. Directly after this she struck with a loud noise against the stone pier. Ben sprang to his feet, and with the boat-hook did his best to fend off the boat, shouting at the same time to the crew to come to his assistance; but they were too much occupied with what was going forward on shore to listen to him. Still he continued to exert himself to the uttermost, for he saw that, if he did not do so, the boat would be dashed to pieces. Again and again he shouted, till he was almost worn out with his labours. He might at any moment have jumped on shore, and left the boat to her fate; but he never thought of doing so. While he was thus engaged, he heard his name called, and, looking up, he saw the good-natured face of Mr Manners, who was watching him from the quay above.

"Why, boy Hadden, how comes it that you are left in the boat alone?" he asked. "Where are the rest?"

"There, sir," said Ben, pointing to where a few were to be seen.

The midshipman ran towards them, shouting out at the same time. They came, at length, very unwillingly.

"See, you have allowed the boat to be almost stove in!" exclaimed the generally quiet young midshipman. "Jump in, now, and keep her off. Where are the rest?"

The men, after getting into the boat, were silent for some time. The midshipman repeated the question.

"Just round the end of that street," said one of the men. "Shall I go and call them, sir? What keeps them, I don't know."

"No," answered the midshipman firmly. "We will pull off a short distance, and wait for them. If they do not come down immediately, I will go on board without them."

The officer was just about to utter the words, "Give way!" when the missing men were seen hurrying down, with uneven steps, towards the quay. The boat put in, and took them on board. Their countenances were flushed, and their manner wild; but they did not venture to speak much. The midshipman saw that they were endeavouring to conceal something, as they took their seats. "Heave those bottles overboard!" he exclaimed suddenly, when they had got a little way from the quay.

The men hesitated. "Not till they are empty," cried one. "Not till we have had what is in them," exclaimed another, putting a bottle to his lips.

The midshipman, a spirited lad, sprang from his seat, and, passing the intervening men, with a boat-stretcher which he had seized dashed the bottle from the man's lips ere a drop could have been drunk. This so exasperated the already tipsy sailor, that he flung himself on the young officer, and, seizing him in his arms, threw him overboard.

Ben, though not in time to prevent this, jumped from the boat, holding on by one of the tiller-ropes, and grasped his young officer by the collar. "Haul us in, mates!" he cried. "You won't surely add murder to what that man has done!"

Even the worst men were somewhat sobered when they saw what had happened, and the other man who had the bottle to his lips stopped drinking; and, fearful of consequences to themselves, they began to haul the officer and Ben together on board.

"Quick! quick, mates! or it will be too late!" cried the coxswain, who had remained on the quay, though he had been guilty of letting the other men go.

A dark object was seen in the water. It darted towards them.

"A shark! a shark!" was the cry.

Ben quickly sprang into the boat; but barely was Mr Manners hauled on board than a flash of white appeared, a huge mouth opened and closed again with a loud snap, and a shark darted away, disappointed of its prey. Even the most drunken of the men were sobered, and the bottles of spirit they had procured at so much risk were thrown overboard. The midshipman quickly recovered.

"They are all gone, sir," said the coxswain in a humble tone. "The men hope that you won't say anything about what has happened."

"I would gladly avoid doing so, so far as I am myself concerned, although, no thanks to Dick Nolan, I am a living man, instead of a dead one in the body of a shark; but discipline must be maintained. I should be neglecting my duty if I did not report those who disobeyed orders. I shall speak of you in no vindictive spirit, and it will not be my fault if the man who threw me into the water receives the punishment which is justly his due: that punishment would be nothing short of death—remember that, my men! I have been taught by a Book, which I wish that you all would read, to forgive my enemies and those who injure me; and therefore I will, for the sake of our loving Saviour, endeavour to save Nolan's life."

The men hung down their heads. This was a very different style of address from what they were accustomed to. No one expected it; even Ben, who had frequently been with Mr Manners, did not. The most hardened felt ashamed of themselves; they were certain that the young officer would not injure them if he could help it, but they also knew that he must report them.

At length the boat reached the ship, and Mr Manners went into the cabin to give an account of the mission on which he had been sent on shore. Ben felt very anxious for the boat's crew; and the culprits, especially, felt very anxious for themselves. Ben forgot all about himself, and he did not suppose that he was likely to gain credit for the part he had acted. He was therefore very much surprised when he was sent for into the cabin.

"I find, Hadden, that you have behaved admirably on two occasions to-day, once in staying by the boat when the proper boat-keepers had left her, and preventing her from being stove in; and secondly, in jumping into the sea and saving Mr Manners when he fell overboard. I wish you to know how highly I approve of your conduct, and will consider how I can best reward you."

Ben was highly pleased at hearing this. He kept pulling away at the front lock of his hair, and thanking the captain, till he was told that he might leave the cabin.

Seamen generally know what has taken place among each other, even when the officers do not. Tom soon heard all that had occurred, and told his father. It was reported the next day that the captain proposed flogging three of the men who had been on shore with Mr Manners. Then it was known that several of the boat's crew were down with a severe fever, and it was reported that the captain knew that there was a fever on shore, and that therefore he had not given leave to the men to go as they had been accustomed to do. Nolan, who had thrown Mr Manners overboard, was the very worst of them. It was said that he was talking very frantically, and accusing himself of the deed. In this dreadful state he continued raving for two days, when he was silent from exhaustion, and died. The captain, hoping to prevent the spread of the fever among the crew, put to sea. Many more, however, were taken ill, of whom several died, and were buried at sea.

One day, Mr Martin called Ben and Tom into his cabin. "Now, boys, I just want to point out to you what you must remember to the end of your days; that is, the terrible effects of disobedience. Those poor fellows whose corpses we have lowered overboard, I daresay, thought that they were doing no great harm when they ran off to the grog-shop. They knew, of course, that they were disobeying the orders of Mr Manners, the midshipman in command of the boat; but they said to themselves, 'Oh, he is only a midshipman, no harm can come of it. We shall be back before he is, and he need know nothing about the matter.' They forgot that the midshipman was acting under the orders of the captain, and the captain under those of the Government of our country, and that Governments and authorities were instituted by God for the well-being and happiness of the community. They thought that they were committing a little sin, but they were in reality guilty of a great crime. See the result. One of them nearly committed murder, and if he had lived, and the captain had been informed of what he had done, he would have been hung. I know all about it, though the crew think I don't. Then they catch the fever, bring it aboard, some of them lose their own lives, and they risk the lives of all the ship's company. Just in the same way people go on in the world. God has given us orders what we are to do, and what we are not to do. How do we act? We neglect to do what He has commanded us to do, and do the very things He has told us not to do, saying all the time to ourselves, 'It is only a little sin, it is only a slight disobedience; so slight, God won't notice it; no harm can come of it.' That is one of Satan's most cunning and most successful devices for destroying the souls of men. He tried it with Adam and Eve, and has tried it on all their descendants ever since, and will try it as long as he 'goes about like a roaring lion, seeking whom he may devour.' Oh, boys, remember that 'not a sparrow falls to the ground' but God sees it, and that He therefore knows all that you do; and that, though a sin may appear a trifle in your sight, it is not a trifle in God's sight, for He abhors all sin. 'He cannot look on iniquity.'"

Tom looked very grave when his father spoke, and felt very serious. Ben clearly understood and remembered the important lesson given him, and prayed silently that he might always make use of it when, temptation should come in his way. He was very happy, and he knew it, in being in a ship with such good men as Mr Charlton and Mr Martin, to whom he now found that he might add Mr Manners. These men, though only a few among many, had a great effect on the mass, and helped to leaven in some degree the whole ship's company. Ben himself produced a good effect not only on Tom, but among the other boys of the ship, and even with many of the men, though he was not aware of it, and would not have talked about it if he had been.

In consequence of the fever, the frigate did not go back to Valparaiso, but stood away to the northward, looking in at other ports along the coast where any British merchantmen were to be found. It is thus England protects her commerce, by showing the inhabitants of the various ports in the world to which her merchants trade, that she has the power to punish those who may venture to ill-treat them; her consuls and any other authorities are supported; and any seamen or other British subjects who misbehave themselves on board English ships can be brought to punishment. If British subjects break the laws of the country in which they are residing, they are left to be punished according to those laws. It is, however, the duty of the consul, supported by the authority of the captain of a man-of-war, to see that they are not punished except justly, according to those laws.

Callao, the port of Lima, the capital of Peru, was the last place on the west of America at which the frigate touched. She anchored in a large bay, guarded by forts, and opposite the modern town of Callao, which stands near the beach. Upwards of a hundred years ago a fearful earthquake occurred, which shook Lima to the ground; and a huge wave rolling in towards the shore at the same time, overwhelmed the old town of Callao, and destroyed the greater part, if not the whole, of the inhabitants.

Peru was taken by the Spaniards three hundred years ago from the native Indians, who lived happily under their own princes and chiefs. The latter were treated with the greatest cruelty and injustice by their conquerors, and compelled to work in the silver and copper mines which exist along the whole range of the Andes. The Spaniards were, in their turn, dispossessed of the government of the country by the

W. H. G. Kingston

descendants of the early settlers, who were assisted by the natives and the people descended from natives and Spaniard. Unhappily, the Roman Catholic religion is established throughout the whole of Chili and Peru, for the history of the two countries is nearly the same; and the people have the characteristics which are to be found wherever that religion prevails. The great mass are ignorant and superstitious; their priests, of whom there are great numbers, grossly impose on their credulity.

The mines, as from the first, are worked by the natives, who are, however, from their delicate constitutions, so unfitted for that sort of labour that they have rapidly decreased in numbers. The consequence is, that many of the mines have been closed for want of hands to work them.

While the Ajax lay at Callao, Captain Bertram heard that, shortly before, an expedition of a dozen or more vessels had been fitted out to entrap and carry off the natives of the various islands of the Pacific, for the purpose of making them work in the mines of Peru. What mattered it to these wretches whether the islanders they proposed to enslave were Christians and civilised, or cannibal savages? They would have preferred the former as more likely to be docile under the treatment to which they proposed to subject them. At first Captain Bertram would scarcely believe that people professing to be civilised and Christians could be guilty of an act of such atrocious barbarity. He remembered, however, who these Chilians are; that in their dispositions and education they differ in no way from Spaniards, and that the Spanish have been to the last the most active agents in the African slave-trade. Those who know the high state of civilisation of which the natives of Eastern Polynesia are capable, and the remarkable fitness of their minds for receiving the truths of the gospel, will naturally feel unmitigated horror at the thought of their being made the victims of so abominable a scheme. This was especially the feeling of Mr Charlton when he heard the account, and he resolved to use every exertion to capture the slavers, and to bring their crews to justice.

W. H. G. Kingston

CHAPTER NINE

ADVENTURES AMONG THE ISLANDS

The Ajax had remained at Callao in order that Captain
Bertram might obtain more information respecting the
slaving expedition of which he had received notice. All he
could learn, however, was that a dozen or more vessels had
sailed, fully armed, with stores for a long cruise, and a larger
quantity of rice and other provisions than could be required
by their crews. Where they had gone no one could tell.
Probably the islands they were to attack were left to the
choice of their commanders.

On putting to sea, the Ajax steered to the westward. As the
frigate approached the numerous groups of islands which lay
in her course, it became necessary to keep a very bright look-
out, by day as well as by night. The first group consisted of
low coral islands, which rise but a few feet above the water.

Ben was anxious to make himself useful as before, and was
continually at the masthead, when his watch was over,
looking out for land. One day, when he was as usual aloft,
turning his eyes round in every direction, he saw right ahead
what seemed to be a grove of trees rising directly out of the
water. He reported what he saw. Sail was immediately
shortened, and the lead hove, and, as the ship sailed on, the

lead was again frequently hove.

"It is the Minerva coral island," Ben heard the captain observe to Mr Charlton, after he and the master had been looking over the chart.

As the ship rose and fell with the swell of the ocean, the trees were now seen and now again lost sight of alternately for some time; this had a very curious effect. As the frigate drew near, a white sandy beach was seen, and, higher up, a belt of land of a light clay colour, on which grew a few shrubs not more than fifteen feet high, above which towered the pandanus, cocoa-nut, and palms. The whole island was about ten miles long, and a mile and a half wide, the centre part being occupied by a lagoon, or lake, of smooth deeply blue water, thus leaving a belt of land not more than six hundred feet across. This lagoon had no opening or entrance to it, but Ben heard that the lagoons of most of the coral islands have a communication with the sea, so that boats and canoes can enter. Outside the island, at some little distance, rose a second or outer reef, over which the sea flowed at high water. This served in heavy gales, when the waves rolled in furious to break their force, and to protect the shore over which they might otherwise have swept, carrying away the trees and shrubs which made it a fit habitation for man.

Mr Martin gave Ben and Tom an account of the way these coral islands are formed. "Coral, you will understands is made by very small sea insects, who form it for their habitation," he observed. "God has given them the instinct to build in certain ways and places, just, as if they knew what they were about, and that they were building up an island fit to be inhabited by human beings. They seem to choose the tops of rocks from one hundred to two hundred fathoms below the surface, for the foundation of their structure. They have toiled on for ages, placing storey upon storey, till the

W. H. G. Kingston

surface has been reached, when they have been compelled to cease; for out of the water, whence they draw their materials—their bricks and mortar, so to speak—they can do nothing. The outer edge breaks the force of the sea, but not altogether. Enough strength is exerted during storms to tear off the outer edge of the coral, and to throw it on the top of the wall. Seaweed and driftwood and dead fish are next thrown up on it, which, when they decay, form soil. Birds next come and rest on the island, and further enrich the soil. They bring seeds of grass and small shrubs at first, and afterwards of larger trees, which take root and spring up, and in their turn, when they decay, form more earth to nourish a larger species of trees, such as the tall palms, and cocoa-nut, and pandanus, which we have seen growing on them. The sandy beach is formed of the broken coral and shells, ground small by the constant action of the waves. I have heard that the lagoons are often very deep, so that the island is exactly like a circular wall built up from the bottom of the sea, or rather from a rock far down in it."

Mr Martin promised the boys that he would tell them more about other islands which they were likely to visit another time. He had also with him some most interesting accounts of the progress which the missionaries had made among the heathen in those seas, which he promised also to give them.

People were seen on the shore, though no habitations were visible, and Captain Bertram wished to communicate with them. While the frigate was hove to, to leeward of the island, two boats were sent on shore under Mr Charlton's command. Ben went in one of them. A native of Tahiti, called Tatai, had been shipped at Callao to act as interpreter, as without one very little intercourse could have been held with the natives. Ben had told him all about Ned, and how he hoped to find him on one of the islands they expected to visit Tatai said that he must not be too sanguine, as it was very like looking for a pearl in a bed of oysters, though there were great numbers of white men scattered about among the islands, and even living among the most savage natives. He promised, however, to make inquiries, and to help on his object as far as he had the power.

The boats had to coast along for some time before an entrance through the reef could be found. The sea dashed against the reef, and, curling over, fell back in a shower of spray. A boat striking it would have been instantly overwhelmed or dashed to pieces. The passage between the two walls of water which thus rose up on either side of the entrance was very narrow. It seemed indeed that the boats could not pass through without the oars touching the rocks. Mr Charlton, however, considered that the passage was practicable, so also did Tatai. Mr Charlton led, and as his boat was cautiously feeling its way, a smooth roller majestically approached the shore. "Give way, lads," he cried. The boat glided on, the water broke with a thundering roar on the reef; but the boat, like an arrow, had shot through and was floating safely within the reef. The other boat immediately followed.

The natives from the shore had been watching these proceedings, and now gathered in considerable numbers on the beach. They were all armed with spears, and showed an evident dislike to holding intercourse with the white people. They nourished their spears, pointed them towards the boats, and made significant gestures for the intruders to depart. Still, as it was important to speak to the poor savages, Mr Charlton pulled towards a ledge of rocks which ran out from the shore, and with a basket full of presents, landed, accompanied by Tatai. The people ran towards him, threatening with their spears as before. He advanced as if to meet them, put down the presents, and then retreated. An old man, who wore a short petticoat of leaves fastened round his waist, and a pandanus leaf hung from his neck as a sign that he was a

W. H. G. Kingston

chief, was in front. He stopped, picked up the handkerchiefs, knives, and trinkets which formed the offering made to him, and, having handed them to his followers, rushed on, gesticulating furiously, towards the English officer. Tatai shouted out that the visitors came as friends, but the only reply he got was, "Go away, go away! we do not want you," spoken in the native tongue.

This was not encouraging. Mr Charlton, however, was not to be defeated. Pulling off to a little distance from the shore, he consulted with Tatai. "If we land without arms and offer them food, that will show that we wish to be friends," he said. Tatai agreed to this, and offered to accompany the lieutenant, provided the boat kept near enough to render them assistance if required.

Again the boat pulled in, and Mr Charlton told Ben that he might land with him, as the savages would see by a boy being of the party that no treachery could be intended. Again the boat touched the beach, at a spot where she could easily be shoved off, and, having deposited his sword and pistols and rifle in the boat, Mr Charlton with his two companions proceeded towards a group of natives who had been watching their proceedings. The natives, instead of coming towards them, seemed to be holding a consultation together. Mr Charlton and his companions, seeing this, sat down, and, taking the provisions out of the basket Ben carried, commenced eating. After a short time, placing the food on a flat rock, and retiring to a little distance, they made signs to the natives to come and eat.

The natives now without hesitation came down, led by their old chief, who took the lion's share of the food, which he seemed to enjoy very much. When the old man had finished eating, Tatai addressed him. He no longer said, "go away," but listened attentively. The interpreter told him that the

English had come to his island as friends; that their only object was to do him good; that they had heard that certain wicked people in vessels had visited some of the islands in their seas, and carried off the natives to make slaves of them; and that, as the English did not like having people made slaves, they were seeking for those bad men to punish them.

The old chief listened attentively to all that was said, and then made a long speech, which Tatai translated. He remarked that everything he had heard was very good; that two suspicious-looking vessels had appeared off the coast not long before; that several boat-loads of armed men had attempted to land; but that, a gale springing up at that moment, they could not effect their purpose, and that the vessels were compelled to bear away.

Mr Charlton, on this, showed the British flag, and told them that, while they behaved well, under that flag they would ever find protection.

The old chief seemed clearly to comprehend what was said. A new light had burst on him. "How is it that your friends are so great and powerful, while I am so poor and miserable?" he asked of Tatai.

"Because my friends worship the great and powerful God, who has given them a Book which makes those who study it wise, while you worship your wretched gods, who are no gods, and cannot help you or make you wise, or do you any good," answered the interpreter promptly.

"Then I should like to learn about your God," said the old chief.

Tatai, in reply, promised that he would try and send some one who would teach them more about the white man's God,

W. H. G. Kingston

and what He desired them to do, and teach them how to pray to Him.

Mr Charlton was much pleased with what Tatai had said, and promised that he would also try to have either a native or English missionary sent to them. He then made more presents to the old chief, made further inquiries about the vessels of the supposed man-stealers, and, after a friendly farewell to the old chief and his companions, pulled back to the ship.

Thus a visit which threatened to prove disastrous, by judicious management gave promise of being productive of great good to the islanders.

After this, the Ajax visited several other islands, searching for the man-stealers. Some were inhabited, others had the remains of huts, altars, and temples, and had been deserted; and on others no signs of human beings could be discovered.

CHAPTER TEN

TELLS ABOUT MISSION WORK

Mr Martin had, as it may be remembered, promised to give Ben and his son an account of the introduction of Christianity among the islands of the Pacific. One day, during a calm, when the ship floated idly on the ocean, her sails scarcely even flapping against the masts, Tom, on going below, declared that it was too hot to read or think or sleep, and that he did not know what he should do with himself.

"It is not too hot to prevent you from listening though, Master Tom," said his father, who did not like to see any one idle from any excuse. "Call Ben Hadden, and I'll tell you and him something which will interest you, or ought to do so, at all events."

Ben soon came, and the boatswain told him and Tom to sit down just outside his cabin, where there was more air than inside.

"Now listen, youngsters; I'm not going to throw my breath away on unwilling ears," he began.

"I am listening, sir," said Ben.

W. H. G. Kingston

"So am I, father," said Tom, "but I can't promise to keep awake if the yarn is a long one."

"Don't let me catch you with more than one eye shut at a time, or I'll be down on you," answered the boatswain. "As I was saying, now listen. You've heard of Captain Cook, the great navigator, who sailed over and across these seas in every direction, and found out many islands not before known to civilised men. His business was to try and discover new lands, and to do any good he could to the inhabitants, by leaving them seeds and plants and animals; but there was nothing in his directions that I know of about teaching them religion. There would not have been time for him to do much, even if he had had any such instructions, unless he had carried out missionaries with him; but in those days missionaries to heathen lands were not so much as thought of in England. You have heard how Cook was killed by the savages of the Sandwich Islands, who have now become the most civilised of all the people of these seas. The descriptions he and his companions gave of the islanders made some Christian people at home think that, if missionaries were sent to them, they might be persuaded to become Christians. The London Missionary Society had just been formed—that was as far back as 1797. The first of their many noble enterprises was to send out twenty-nine missionaries in the ship Duff, commanded by Captain Wilson. The greater number settled at Tahiti, where they were well received by the natives; while others went to Tongatabu, and two of them attempted to commence a mission at Saint Christina, one of the Marquesas. The latter mission was, however, soon afterwards abandoned, and has never since been resumed; and unhappily, as the French have taken possession of the group, there is not much probability of an English Protestant mission being established there, whatever the French Protestants may do.

"At Tahiti many years passed before any fruits of the missionaries' labours were perceived, not indeed till 1813, when some praying natives were discovered, and a church was formed. From that time, however, Christianity spread rapidly, and the converted natives were eager to go forth themselves as missionaries, not only to neighbouring islands, such as the Paumotre, the Austral, and Hervey groups, but to Raratonga and Samoa, and, still farther, to the New Hebrides, Loyalty Islands, and New Caledonia and Penryn Islands.

"The climate of those islands in the Western Pacific, near the equator, is nearly as hurtful to the constitutions of the inhabitants of the eastern part of that ocean as to Europeans, and very many native missionaries have fallen martyrs in the cause of the gospel. In some instances the English missionaries were the first to land, and afterwards to employ native agency; in others, the natives were first sent to a heathen island, and the more highly-educated white men followed, to complete the work commenced by their dark-skinned brethren. In many instances the missionaries had long to wait before they saw the fruit of their labours; in others, the natives at once gladly accepted the glorious tidings of salvation. In very few have missions been ultimately abandoned in consequence of the hostility of the natives in the Eastern Pacific; the Marquesas is the chief exception. In the Western Pacific the natives have been much more hostile to the missionaries. This has arisen in consequence of the treatment they have often received from the crews of whale-ships, and from sandal-wood traders. These men have been known to carry off natives from one island, to make them cut sandal-wood on another inhabited by their mortal foes, and after their task has been accomplished the traders have left the poor wretches there to be butchered, and often eaten, by their enemies, to save themselves the trouble of taking them back and paying them their stipulated reward.

W. H. G. Kingston

"The history of the establishment of Christianity on many of these islands is very interesting. The way in which it was introduced into Raratonga, the largest of the Hervey group, is so in particular. Some natives of that island had been carried away in a whale-ship, and left at Aitutaki. Among them was the niece of the principal chief of the island. At Aitutaki, the great missionary Williams saw them, and, accompanied by them, after a long search, discovered their island. This was in 1823. The unfriendly reception he met with from the savage natives, however, made it impossible for him to remain. Had it not been, indeed, for the exertions of Tapaeru, the niece of the chief, who had been carried away, the native teachers who went on shore would have been murdered. They returned on board; but Papehia, one of their number, as the ship was about to sail away, volunteered to return. Tying a book containing a part of the Scriptures in a handkerchief on his head, and clothed in a shirt and trousers only, this true servant of Christ swam back, full of faith, to the rocks, on which stood several of the savages, brandishing their spears. His heart did not falter; he swam on bravely. He had true faith. He followed your rule, Ben; he was determined to do right, whatever was to come of it. He knew that it was right to carry the gospel to these poor savages; he would succeed, or perish in the attempt. Tapaeru from the first protected him, and obtained for him the support of her relations. This enabled him to speak openly to the people, who soon became eager to listen to the wonderful things he had to narrate. Still, he had much opposition to contend with. Tinomana, a powerful chief, was the first man of influence to give up his idols.

"Another native teacher afterwards joined Papehia; and in two years and a half, under the superintendence of these two native teachers,—themselves born heathens, and brought up in the darkness of idolatry, till called into the marvellous light of the gospel,—the whole of the population of that large island became professedly Christian. It was here that, soon after this, Mr Williams built his vessel, the Messenger of Peace, in which he sailed over so large a part of the Pacific. There are now numerous churches, schools, and a training college, from which many native missionaries have gone forth to preach the gospel in far distant islands.

"The conversion of the inhabitants of the Sandwich Islands was still more extraordinary. From the time that Captain Cook was killed on their shores, they had been looked on as among the most savage of the people of the Pacific. The Sandwich Islands, the largest of which is Hawaii, were ruled by a chief of great talent, who had made himself king of the whole group, and was called Tamehameha the First. He had entreated Captain Vancouver, who visited his territories in 1793, to send him Christian missionaries. No attention, however, was paid to this request. His son Rihoriho, who became king in 1820, seeing the utter folly of the religion of his ancestors, without being even urged to do so by foreigners, of his own accord threw off the gods of his people, burnt the idols and their temples, and upset the priesthood, and the whole system connected with it. In this extraordinary proceeding he was supported by the high priest himself, who acknowledged, when appealed to, that the gods they had hitherto worshipped were of no power, and that there was but one God in heaven, the same whom the white men worshipped.

"It was at this juncture that a band of missionaries arrived from the United States, sent out by the American Board of Missions. They were cordially welcomed by the king, most of his chiefs, and the people. Schools were established, churches built, and in a few years the whole of the people became nominally Christians, many of them really so; and civilisation advanced with rapid strides. Among no people, probably, has it made so much progress in so short a time.

W. H. G. Kingston

Still, I believe that among the Society Islands, at Raratonga, and other islands of the Hervey group, true Christianity more extensively prevails.

"The people of Savage Island, who were said to be among the fiercest and most barbarous of the natives of Polynesia, were converted much in the same way as those of Raratonga, and they are now simple-minded Christians, earnest, quiet, and well-behaved.

"In the large island of Tongatabu, and its adjacent islands, great disappointment was encountered by the first missionaries, who were ultimately driven away. In 1820, the Wesleyan Missionary Society sent missionaries there, and by their means the king, George, and the whole population have professed Christianity. The two societies together have laboured in the beautiful islands of Samoa, to the north; and there also Christianity has been generally established.

"Wonderful, also, is the change which has been brought about in a few years in Fiji, a large and beautiful group of islands lying to the west of Tonga. The inhabitants are nearly black, and a very fine and intelligent race of men; but they were even more addicted to cannibalism than the New Zealanders, and their customs were of the most revolting and cruel description. Thackombau, the greatest chief among them, was also a fierce cannibal. Fully aware of the character of the people, a band of Wesleyan missionaries landed on their shores, and by great perseverance have succeeded in bringing over a large number of the population to a knowledge of the truth, including the king himself and all his family; while the practice of cannibalism is almost, if not completely, extirpated.

"The numerous groups of islands to the north of New Zealand are known as Melanesia. The Presbyterian and

London Missionary Societies have for a considerable time been at work in some of these islands. It was on one of them (Erromanga) that Williams met his death, and that Mr Murray and some native missionaries were murdered, while many have died of fever. They have, however, not laboured in vain, and the inhabitants of more than one island have abandoned idol-worship. To these groups, also, the Church of England, established in New Zealand, has turned its attention, under the direction of the Bishop of New Zealand, who made several voyages among them. Bishop Pattison, with the title of Bishop of Melanesia, has been especially appointed to superintend the work of evangelisation connected with them. A vessel called the Southern Cross makes a cruise twice a year among them. In the spring, she collects young men from all the islands and carries them to New Zealand, where they receive instruction in a college established for that purpose. As they can no more stand the cold climate of New Zealand in the winter than Europeans can stand the heat of their summer, in the autumn the Southern Cross carries them back to their own islands, where they instruct their countrymen in the religious knowledge and the arts they have learned during their absence. The French have sent Roman Catholic missionaries to several of these groups. They have taken possession of Tahiti; and have established colonies there, on the coast of New Guinea, and in the Marquesas. At Tahiti, the English Protestant missionaries were for a time prohibited from preaching, and compelled to leave the island. The greater number of the people, supported by the queen, remained firm to their Protestant principles; and at length a French Evangelical Society sent out Protestant pastors, and the people have now perfect religious liberty, though they remain subject to France.

"Notwithstanding the large number of islands in which Christianity has been firmly established, it is calculated that there are two hundred and fifty inhabited islands still sunk in the darkness of idolatry and savageism, so that there remains a very large amount of work to be done. There, I have given you a short account of missionary work in the Pacific. Another day I will get a chart, and show you the places I have spoken about. I will then tell you more respecting them. You will like especially to hear of Savage Island, or Niue, which I understand we are to visit, to inquire about some natives who, it is reported, have been carried away by the Chilian slavers."

Ben thanked Mr Martin very much for the information he had given him and Tom, and begged that he would give them a further account of Savage Island, as he had kindly offered to do.

CHAPTER ELEVEN

MORE EXPLORATIONS AND ADVENTURES

Shortly after the events mentioned in a former chapter, the Ajax came in sight of a cluster of mountains, rising, it seemed, directly out of the sea, to the height of four thousand feet. It was the island of Raratonga, of which Mr Martin had told Ben. It is surrounded by a curious barrier-reef of solid block coral, thirty-five miles in circumference, and from a quarter of a mile to half a mile broad. At high water it is completely covered to a depth of four or six feet, but at low water it is almost bare. This vast reef prevents the sea from breaking against the island. Outside the reef there is no anchorage ground, as no cable could fathom the depth. Inside, the water is smooth and beautifully clear, but no ship of any size can pass through the reef. There are several passages for canoes and boats, and one for a vessel of forty-five tons. This is, however, a very great advantage to the inhabitants in a social point of view, as it prevents the establishment of a seaport town in their island, while, at the same time, they can enjoy intercourse with the rest of the world. This was the very island of which Mr Williams had heard, and which he so long looked for before he found it. Here the missionary Papehia landed alone, trusting in Jehovah, among its then savage inhabitants. It was here the great missionary Williams spent many months, and built single-handed the schooner—the Messenger of Peace mentioned before—in which he crossed over so many thousand miles of the Pacific Ocean, to carry the glad tidings of great joy to many of the numerous islands scattered over it. It was here that a fierce chief, Tinomana, became a humble, lowly-minded Christian, and died strong in the faith. This is the island, the inhabitants of which were among the fiercest of all the isles of the Pacific, and are now among the most consistent and truest Christians. It has sent out more missionaries than any other to convert the heathen of the isles of the Pacific. It contains a training college for missionaries, with numerous churches and schools. The houses of the inhabitants are well-built, neat, and clean; and it is hardly too much to say that, in the same space, and among an equal number of people living together in any part of the world, a larger proportion of true and consistent Christians will not be found.

As soon as the frigate hove to, near the land, several canoes came off to welcome the well-known flag. The natives were decently dressed in shirts and trousers, with straw hats; and their manner was particularly quiet and at the same time cheerful. They offered to bring off any provisions which might be required; but the captain wished himself to go on shore, and said that he could then purchase what he wanted. Two whalers were at the time standing off and on the land, while their boats were on shore. Ben was glad to find that three boats from the frigate were going on shore, to one of which he belonged. A native pilot in his boat led the way, the captain's gig following; but, as the wind was light and the tide high, there was no difficulty in passing through the barrier, and, once inside, the boats were in smooth water.

The officer on landing was met by a respectable-looking native, who announced himself as the salesman of the station, putting out his right hand, and saying, "*Ria-ora-na*!"

(Blessings on you.) The officers were then conducted to the market-house, where there were stores of bananas, yams, pumpkins, potatoes, cocoa-nuts, fowls, and various other articles. The purser of the frigate then stated the quantity of provisions he required. The salesman informed him of the current price, a calculation was made, the money was paid, and the salesman undertook to engage native boats, in which everything was taken off in excellent condition.

The captain first visited the mission establishment. It consisted of a centre building, and a great number of small houses. These were the residences of the married students; every single student had a room to himself. Nearly two hundred students have been educated at the college. A very important part of the establishment is the printing-press, which supplies with a number of valuable works, not only Raratonga, but numerous other islands of the Pacific where the dialect of the inhabitants is understood. The students also consist, not only of natives of the Hervey Islands, but young men from far distant places. In each village there are schools and churches and native pastors. Children also are brought from other islands to the chief school, under the English missionary, to receive instruction. Thus from this once savage country the true light now shines forth over a wide circle of the Pacific—that light brought to those shores by the once heathen Papehia!

When the boats got back to the frigate, Ben found that the captain of one of the whalers, the Grand Turk, was on board. Captain Judson—that was his name—was well-known to Mr Martin, who had once sailed with him. He was waiting to see Captain Bertram, to prefer some request or other. He was evidently a rough style of man, and was complaining much of the way he had been treated the day before, which was Sunday.

"Two boats were sent on shore, but none of the people were to be seen," said Captain Judson. "There were a number of neat, whitewashed houses in rows, some way from the beach, and near them three larger buildings. One had a tower. After waiting for some time, people came streaming out of the door of the building with the tower, all neatly dressed in cottons or native cloths.

"'Why, they look just as if they were coming out of church,' said one of my men, who had never been out in these parts before, and thought all the people were savages and cannibals. After some time, a white gentleman appeared in a black dress. 'And there comes the parson, I do declare!' he added."

"The first mate, who had charge of the party, on this went up to the gentleman, and told him what we had come for.

"'I am very glad to hear it,' said the gentleman. 'I have no doubt that to-morrow morning the people will bring you all you require.'"

"'To-morrow won't do—we want the things to-day; we must be off again this evening,' said the mate, in an angry tone, for of course he was vexed."

"'I will tell the people what you say; but they have been taught to remember the Sabbath-day to keep it holy, and I do not think that they will supply you, unless you are starving, or have scurvy for want of vegetables, and then I am certain that they will give you all you require,' answered the missionary, who then spoke to several of the people; and a young native came forward, and in very good English told the mate that he was the interpreter, and would be glad to attend him. The mate thought that he could manage him, and was very much surprised to find that no trading could be allowed that day.

"'But our people may go on shore and amuse themselves?' said the mate."

"'No,' answered the young native. 'Too often the crews of whalers have come on shore, and have set a bad example to our people, who think a great deal about white men. We allow no strangers to wander about our island on the Sabbath.'"

"'Then your people will come off to us, as they do at other islands!' said the mate."

"'No, no, no,' answered the young native, with a grave look. 'Such things were, but they were very bad; we have learned better now.'"

"On hearing this, the mate came away, abusing the missionaries for having taught the natives such things. It is fair to say, however, that, as he was leaving the beach to come on board, a number of natives appeared with baskets of cooked vegetables and fruits, enough for the dinner of the whole crew. All the families near had given up some from their own store. I was in a hurry to be off, and sent on shore in the evening, offering to pay double for what we wanted; but the people were still obstinate.

"'To-morrow morning we will trade gladly,' was the answer."

"From every cottage came the sound of prayer, or voices singing hymns or psalms. Certainly these people, little better than savages as they are, do keep the Sunday very strictly. I never saw it kept like that elsewhere. Some people who care about those things might say that they put us to shame."

"The next morning, when we stood in at daybreak, the vessel was soon surrounded by canoes, full of all the provisions we wanted; and we were told that, if we required, men would be ready to help us fill our water-casks. Still, I don't like to be put out as we have been, and I shall go when next we want fresh provisions to one of the islands where things are carried on in the old-fashioned way."

Captain Judson had come on board to get some lime-juice, the best thing to prevent scurvy. He said that he had bought a good supply of what was called lime-juice; but, when the surgeon examined it, which he did when, in spite of the men using it, the scurvy appeared among them, he found that it was some common acid, of no use whatever. How horribly wicked were the manufacturers who could thus, in their greed for grain, knowingly destroy the health and lives of seamen who depended on their useless mixtures for preserving them from one of the most terrible maladies to which those who make long voyages are subject! Whether or not the owners of the Grand Turk had paid less for this mixture than they would have done for good lime-juice is difficult to say; but it might certainly have cost the whole crew their lives, and it certainly cost them the loss of some hundreds of pounds while the ship was sailing away to procure vegetables, with a third of her crew on the sick-list, instead of catching whales.

Captain Judson obtained the lime-juice for which he had come; indeed, the Ajax had brought out a quantity on purpose to supply ships which might require it. He then took his departure, and, whatever he might have thought, the rest of the crew continued to grumble greatly at not having been allowed to go on shore and amuse themselves, as they called it, and expressed a hope that it was the last missionary island they should touch at in their voyage.

The captain of the other whaler afterwards came on board. He was a wiser man than Captain Judson. He said that he made a point of visiting those islands where missionaries were established, as he was certain that he could then trust the people, whereas among the heathen islands he lived always in dread of having his boats' crews cut off, as had happened to many others to his knowledge.

On leaving Raratonga, the Ajax bore away for Savage Island, or Niue. Captain Cook describes the inhabitants as among the most savage of those he encountered. As his boat drew near to the shore, they rushed down towards him with the ferocity of wild boars to drive him away. In consequence of the behaviour of the natives, he gave it the name of Savage Island. Subsequent visitors, for many years after that, fully confirmed the account he gave of the people.

The Ajax came off the island about five days after leaving Raratonga. The two islands are about of an equal size, but in other respects are very unlike each other, as the highest part of Savage Island is not more than a hundred feet above the level of the sea. Instead of the savages Captain Cook encountered, and those who, as late as 1846, would have been on the coast, several canoes, with well-dressed, quiet-looking natives, came off to the ship. They all wore sad countenances, for they had indeed a tale of woe to tell. Captain Bertram inquired what had happened to them.

"Sad, sad," answered the interpreter. "Early one morning a strange ship appeared off the coast. We thought nothing of that, as many have come and gone and brought missionaries to us, and others have called for vegetables and other produce, for which they have paid. This one had no flag to tell us whence she came, or what was her object in coming. As soon as we had finished our usual morning prayer, several canoes put off with fruits and vegetables to take to

W. H. G. Kingston

the strangers, and to learn what else they required. Among those who went off were some of our leading men, the lawmakers and law-enforcers of our island. There were thirty or more church members, a deacon, and many candidates, most of them among our most promising young men. They were at once welcomed on board, and treated with great attention. Suddenly the white crew rushed in among them with clubs, knocked down all on deck, and then they fired their guns at those attempting to escape in their canoes. Several of the people in them were shot or drowned when the canoes were destroyed. The people in most of the canoes were so astonished that they did not even attempt to escape. Instantly they were ordered on board the strange ship, which continued firing at the retreating canoes. Three only of these got away, and one of them conveyed the corpse of Simeon, a church member, shot through the head. The stranger, finding that no other canoes would go off from this part of our island, sailed away, with our fathers and brothers, and our other Christian friends, on board. Our hearts were bowed down with grief; but we prayed earnestly that we might forgive our enemies, and that God, in His great mercy, would change their hearts. (A fact.) We would not curse them, we would not pray that God would wreak His vengeance on their heads; for are we not told that, as we forgive our enemies, so alone can we ask God to forgive us?"

The slaver, it appeared, had sailed along the coast, the natives being decoyed on board wherever met with, and then she had gone off to other islands to pursue the same nefarious system. Captain Bertram went on shore to make further inquiries. He found that all the inhabitants had professed Christianity, and that, though not so advanced as the natives of Raratonga, who have been so much longer tinder instruction, they were making fair progress in Christian, as well as in secular, knowledge and civilisation. As no time was to be lost, the Ajax again sailed in pursuit of the slaver.

She first stood across to Samoa, in the direction of which the slaver had been seen to steer. She looked in at several of the ports of that fine group of islands, and here also gained information of the transactions of the slavers, for several had appeared, and succeeded in kidnapping many natives. It was supposed that some of these slave-ships had sailed to the north-east, purposing to visit the groups of islands lying on either side of the equator. Many islands were touched at, and inquiries made. A sharp look-out too was kept, for all were eager, from the captain to the youngest boy on board, to catch the miscreants who were outraging all laws, human and divine, in thus carrying off the innocent natives into slavery.

W. H. G. Kingston

CHAPTER TWELVE

THE FRIGATE IN DANGER

One day, a sail was sighted, becalmed. The frigate carried the breeze up to her. At first it was hoped that she was a slaver. She proved, however, to be a whaler, the Grand Turk, whose captain had come on board the Ajax off Raratonga. As Captain Bertram wished to make inquiries of Captain Judson respecting the slavers, he invited him on board. The captain of the whaler seemed very much out of spirits. Before he went away, Mr Martin had a long talk with him, and inquired what was the matter.

"Why, Martin, I am afraid that I have been a very sinful and foolish man," he answered. "You shall hear what has occurred. You know how I used to abuse the missionaries, and say that they spoilt all the people they got among, and that I would never visit another missionary island if I could help it. Wishing to get more vegetables, we made for an island known to be heathen. We anchored in a sheltered bay, where I knew that the people would give us all we wanted for a mere song. We had soon plenty of natives on board, men and women. They danced and sang, and drank as much rum as our men would give them. I need not describe the scenes which took place. I must confess, what I now see to be the truth, that we have no business to call ourselves

Christians, or civilised people, while we allow such things to occur. Yet they were not worse than have been carried on at many islands, ever since our whalers came to these seas.

"The next day a quantity of provisions were brought down to the beach, and, thinking the people so inclined to be friendly, I let a number of our men go on shore. I was in my cabin when I heard a shot. I ran on deck, and saw our men running towards the boats. Now and then they stopped and fired at a large band of natives, who were following them with clubs and spears. Another body of natives were rushing down on one side to try and cut off our men, and great numbers of others were launching canoes in all directions. I had very little hope that our men would escape, but to help them I had an anchor and cable carried out astern, by hauling on which we brought our broadside to bear on the boats. Our guns were then fired at the second party of natives of which I have spoken. This stopped them, or the whole of our men would have been cut off. We could not go to their assistance, as we had to remain on board to defend the ship from the canoes, which were now coming towards her. Two of our men had been killed before our eyes; the greater number were shoving off the boats. They had just got them afloat, when the savages, gaining courage, charged them. Two more of our poor fellows were knocked on the head. The rest jumped into the boats and pulled off from the beach. They had no time to fire. The canoes made chase after them. All we could do was to fire at the canoes with our big guns and muskets as they came on, hotly chasing the boats till they got alongside. The men climbed up the sides by the ropes we hove to them. We had barely time to hoist in the boats when the savages in vast numbers came round us, uttering the most fearful shrieks and cries. While some of my men kept them off with lances, and by firing down on them, others hove up the anchor and went aloft to loose sails. There was fortunately a fresh breeze off shore; our topsails filled, and we stood out of the bay, while the savages kept close round us, hoping, no doubt, that we should strike on a reef and become their easy prey. We had to fly here and there to keep them from gaining the deck, for as soon as one was driven back another took his place. Not till we were well outside the reef did they give up the attempt to take the ship. Not only had we lost the four men killed on the beach, but two others had been cut off in the boats, and several of those who got on board were badly wounded. I suspect that the savages had from the first intended to take the ship, for I could not make out that our men had given them any special cause of quarrel. I was thankful when we were well free of them, and I must confess to you, Martin, that you were right when you advised me to visit a Christian island instead of a heathen one. I cannot get over the loss of those poor fellows. It has been a severe lesson to me, and I am, I believe, a wiser man."

"I am very sorry for the loss of your people, Mr Judson, and yet God will rule the event for your good if you continue to see it in the light you now do," observed Mr Martin. "The example which our so-called Christian seamen have set to the natives of these islands has been fearful. Their behaviour has created one of the chief difficulties to the progress of the gospel with which the missionaries have had to contend. It is, humanly speaking, surprising that they have made any progress at all. Were it not indeed that God's hand has been in the work through the agency of the Holy Spirit, it is impossible that they could have succeeded."

Captain Judson did not, perhaps, clearly comprehend the meaning of all Mr Martin said; but he thanked him cordially for his remarks, and returned on board his ship with several religious and other books for his crew, and among them a Bible, which he confessed that he had not before got on board.

"What!" exclaimed Ben, when he heard this from Mr Martin; "a ship go to sea without a Bible! How can the people get on? how can they do their duty? I am afraid they must forget to say their prayers."

"You are right, Ben," observed Mr Martin; "there are very many ships that go to sea without Bibles, and the crews very often forget their duty to God and man. In my younger days, indeed, there were very few which took Bibles, and the exception was to find one. A praying, Bible-reading captain and ship's company was a thing almost unknown."

Ben, who had carefully preserved his Bible, prized it sincerely, and read it every day, was surprised to hear this. There were a good many men also on board the Ajax who had Bibles, and read them frequently. Sometimes some of the other boys had laughed at Ben when they found him reading his Bible, but he did not mind them, and went on reading steadily as before.

The account of the cruel way in which the natives had been kidnapped by the Peruvian slavers made everybody on board the Ajax eager to catch some of them. Night and day bright eyes were ever on the watch in different parts of the ship. This was especially necessary in those seas, where rocks and reefs abound; and though they are far better known than in Lord Anson's days, yet there are many parts but imperfectly explored.

Wherever the ship touched, Ben made his usual anxious inquiries for Ned. He, as before, frequently heard of Englishmen living with the savages; but they did not answer to the description of his brother. Still he had hopes that he should find him. Ben remembered his father's advice, and acted up to it: "Do right, whatever comes of it." By so doing he had gained the favour of his captain and all the officers of the ship. Everybody said, "Ben Hadden is a trustworthy fellow; whatever he undertakes to do he does with all his heart, as well as he possibly can."

Ben had consequently plenty to do; but then he reaped the reward of his doing. Sailors are often paid in a glass of grog for any work they do, and they are satisfied; but it was generally known that Ben had a widowed mother, to whom he wished to send home money; and therefore Ben was always paid in coin, and no one grudged it to him, knowing how well it would be employed.

A sailor's life is often a very rough one; but when people are thrown together for a cruise of four years, as were the crew of the Ajax, provided always they have a good captain and judicious officers, they wonderfully rub the rough edges off each other, and a kind and brotherly feeling springs up among them, which often lasts to the end of their lives. Such was the feeling which existed among the officers and ship's company of the Ajax. The officers treated the men with kindness and consideration, and the men obeyed their officers with alacrity.

Hitherto, the Pacific appeared deserving of the name bestowed on it. For many months the Ajax had experienced only fine weather. Undoubtedly, gales had blown, and heavy rains had fallen, during that period; but the ship had sailed across to the west, while they occurred on the eastern part; and afterwards, when she went back towards the American coast, the rains fell and the gales blew on the west. This was, however, not always to be so. One morning, when Ben went on deck to keep his watch, he found the sails hanging down against the masts, and the sea without the slightest ripple to break its mirror-like surface. Every now and then, however, it seemed slowly to rise like the bosom of some huge monster breathing in its sleep, and a smooth low wave heaved up under the ship's keel, and glided slowly away, to be followed at long intervals by other waves of the same character. As they passed, the ship rolled from side to side, or pitched gently into the water, and the sails, hitherto so motionless, flapped loudly against the masts with a sound like that of musketry. The heat was very great; the seamen, overcome by it, went about their various duties with much less than their usual alacrity. The smoke curled slowly up from the galley-funnel, wreathing itself in festoons about the fore-rigging, where it hung, unable, it seemed, to rise higher. Eight bells struck in the forenoon watch, the boatswain's whistle piped to dinner, and the mess-men were seen lazily moving along the deck, with their kids, to the galley-fire, to receive their portions of dinner from the black cook, who, with face shining doubly from the heat which none but a black cook or a German sugar-baker could have endured, was busily employed in serving it out to them. The smell of the good boiled beef or pork—very different from what our sailors once had—seemed to give them appetites, for they hastened back with the smoking viands to their mess-tables slung from the deck above. Here the men sat in rows, with their brightly-polished mess utensils before them, and soon gave proof that the heat had had no serious effect on their health.

It is usual to send all the men below at dinner-time, except those absolutely required to steer and look out, unless the weather is bad, and it is probable that any sudden change may be required to be made in the sails. Most of the officers on this occasion were on deck, slowly walking up and down in the shadow of the sails. Ben and Tom were at their mess-table, laughing and talking and enjoying themselves as boys do in an ordinarily happy ship.

"This is jolly!" observed Tom. "I like a calm, there's so little to do; and it's fair that the sails should have a holiday now and then. They must get tired of sending us along, month after month, as they have to do."

"I do not think they get much rest, after all, even now," said Ben. "Listen how they are flapping against the masts! If they had to do much of that sort of thing, they would soon wear themselves out. What a loud noise they make!"

"Oh yes; but that is only now and then, you see, just to show us that they have not gone to sleep as the wind has done, and are ready for use when we want them," remarked Tom, who had always a ready answer for any observation made by Ben; too ready sometimes, for he thus turned aside many a piece of good advice which his friend gave him. "At all events, the ship can't be getting into any mischief while she is floating all alone out here, away from the land," he added. "If I was the captain, I would turn in and go to sleep till the wind begins to blow again."

Tom did not know how little sleep the captain of a large ship, with the lives of some hundred men confided to him, ventures to take.

Captain Bertram was on deck, walking with Mr Charlton. He stopped, and earnestly looked towards the north-east His keen eye had detected a peculiar colour in the water extending across the horizon in that direction. He pointed it out to Mr Charlton. "What does it seem to you like!" he asked.

"A coral reef, sir. If so, we have been drifting towards it; I should otherwise have seen it in the morning," answered the first lieutenant. "I will, however, go aloft, and make sure what it is."

In spite of the intense heat, Mr Charlton climbed up to the masthead. He carefully scanned the horizon in every direction, and then speedily returned on deck.

"We are nearer to the reef than I had supposed, sir," he said. "We may keep the boats ahead, and somewhat hinder the ship driving so rapidly towards it; but it is evident that a strong current sets in that direction. Had it been at night, we should have struck before we could have seen it."

"Pipe the hands on deck, then, Mr Charlton," answered the captain calmly. "If towing is to serve us, there is no time to be lost."

Mr Martin was sent for, and his shrill whistle soon brought the whole of the crew tumbling up from below, the landsmen and idlers only remaining to stow away the mess things.

The boats were soon lowered and manned, and sent ahead. The hot sun shone down on the men in the boats as they toiled away to keep the ship's head off the reef. It seemed, however, that they rowed to little purpose; for the undulations appeared at shorter intervals, and seemed to send the frigate towards the threatening rocks, on which a surf, not at first perceived, now began to break, forming a white streak across the horizon.

The sails were brailed up, but not furled, in order that they might again be at once set, should a breeze spring up to fill them.

Mr Charlton stood on the forecastle, directing the boats how to pull. Every now and then he cast an anxious eye astern towards the breakers, which continued to rise higher and higher. A cast of the deep-sea lead was taken, but no bottom was found. To anchor was, therefore, impossible. Everybody on board saw the fearful danger in which the frigate was placed. One thing only, it seemed, could save her—a breeze

W. H. G. Kingston

from the direction towards which she was drifting. All eyes, not otherwise employed, were glancing anxiously round the horizon, looking out for the wished-for breeze. Ben and Tom were as active as usual. They remained on board, as only the strongest men were sent into the boats; it was trying even for men. They continued rowing, and, encouraged by their officers, as hard as they had ever before rowed. Suddenly, without a moment's warning, the captain ordered them to return on board.

"Hoist in the boats!" he shouted. "Be smart now, my lads!"

As the boats were being hoisted in, the spoon-drift began to fly across the surface of the hitherto calm ocean, hissing along like sand on the desert. The hitherto smooth undulations now quickly broke up into small waves, increasing rapidly in size and length, with crests of foam crowning their summits.

Directly the boats were secured, the captain shouted, "Hands shorten sail!" The men with alacrity sprang into the rigging and lay out on the yard. The three topsails were closely reefed; all the other square sails were furled. There was a gravity in the look of the captain and officers which, showed that they considered the position in which the ship was placed very dangerous.

Dark clouds now came rushing across the sky, increasing in numbers and density. Even before the men were off the yards, the hurricane struck the frigate. Over she heeled to it, till it seemed as if she would not rise again; but the spars were sound, the ropes good. Gradually she again righted, and, though still heeling over very much, answered her helm, and tore furiously through the foaming and loudly-roaring seas. The captain stood at the binnacle, now anxiously casting his eye along the reef, now at the sails, then at the compass in the binnacle, and once more giving a glance to windward. The ship's company were at their stations ready to obey any order that their officers might issue. Four of the best men were at the wheel, others were on the look-out forward. Not a word was spoken. The wind increased rather than lessened after it first broke on the frigate. Had it been a point more from the eastward, it would have driven her to speedy destruction. As it was, it enabled her to lie a course parallel to the reef; but, notwithstanding this, the leeway she made, caused by the heavy sea and the fury of the gale, continued to drive her towards it, and the most experienced even now dreaded that she would be unable to weather the reef.

The hurricane blew fiercer and fiercer. The frigate heeled over till her lee ports were buried in the foaming, hissing caldron of boiling waters through which she forced her way. It was with difficulty the people could keep their feet. The captain climbed up into the weather mizzen rigging, and there he stood holding on to a shroud, conning the ship, as calm to all appearance as if he had been beating up Plymouth Sound. The men at the helm kept their eyes alternately on him and on the sails, ready to obey the slightest sign he might make. Although the topsails were close reefed, they seemed to bend the spars and masts as they tugged and strained to be free; Mr Martin, the boatswain, kept his eye anxiously on them. Now was the time to prove whether the spars were sound, and, if they were sound, whether the rigging had been properly set up, and if that also was sound throughout. A ship, like a human being, is best tried in adversity; it is not in smooth seas and with gentle breezes that her qualities can be proved, any more than the nature of a man can be ascertained if all goes smoothly and easily with him. Therefore, let no one venture to put confidence in himself, till he has been tossed about by the storms of life, and by that time he will have learned that he is weak and frail under all circumstances, unless sustained by the power of the Holy Spirit, who is alone able to keep him from falling. Ben and Tom had crept up to near where Mr Martin was standing. He saw them exchanging looks with each other.

"There'll be a watery grave for all on board if the spars go," observed Mr Gimblet. "Still, it's a satisfaction to believe that they are as sound sticks as ever grew."

"It's just providential that we set up our rigging only t'other day. If this gale had caught us with it as it was before that time, we might have cried good-bye to our spars, sound as they are," said Mr Martin. "Even now, I wish that the wind would come a point or two more on our quarter; we make great leeway, there's no doubt about that."

Ben and Tom overheard these remarks of the two warrant-officers. Ben fully understood the danger the ship was in, and that before an hour or so was over he and all on board might be in a watery grave; for he saw how impossible it would be for the stoutest ship to hold together if she once struck on the reef to leeward, the fearful character of which had now become more distinct than ever. The sea broke against it with terrific force, rising high up in a wall of water, and then fell curling back on the side from which it came. Not the strongest swimmer could exist for a minute among those breakers. Far away ahead it seemed to extend in one long unbroken line.

The hearts of many on board began to sink; not with unmanly fear, but life was sweet; they had many loved ones in their far distant homes, and they could not but see that long before the frigate could reach the distant point she must drift on the reef. By the loss of one of her sails she would be sent there within a very few minutes. Ben and Tom, young as they were, could not fail clearly to comprehend their danger. Ben did not tremble; he did not give way to tears, or to any weak fears, but he turned his heart to God. To Him the young lad prayed that He would protect his mother: he tried to think of what he had done wrong, that he might earnestly repent; and then he threw himself on the love and mercy of Jesus. "On Thee, O Lord Jesus, on Thee, in Thee I trust," he kept saying. All this time, however, his attention was awake; his eyes were open, and his ears ready to receive any order that might be given. Such is the state of mind, such the way in which many a Christian sailor has met death.

On, on, flew the frigate. It was indeed a time of intense anxiety to all on board. The officers were collected near the captain. A short consultation was held. Some of the men thought that they were going to put the ship about, under the belief that she would lie up taller on the other tack. Should she miss stays, however, and of that there was the greatest danger, her almost instant destruction would be the consequence. No; the captain would not make the attempt. He would trust to a change of wind. Should it come ahead, then there would be time enough to go about; if not, it would be best to stand on. They were in God's hands, not their own. Mr Charlton and the second lieutenant were seen going aloft, with their telescopes at their backs. Eagerly they scanned the line of breakers. It seemed sometimes as if no human being could hold on up there on the mast, with the hurricane raging so furiously around. The evening was drawing on. Should darkness be down on them before they were clear of the reef, what hope of escape could they have? The eyes of the crew were now directed to their two officers aloft. Their lives seemed to depend on the result of their investigations. At length they were seen to be descending. All watched them eagerly as they reached the deck. Their countenances, it was thought, wore a more cheerful aspect than before. The wind had not lessened, nor was there the slightest indication of a

W. H. G. Kingston

change. The men, as has been said, were at their stations, and no one moved. There they would be found to the last, till the ship should strike. There, too, should all Christian men be found when the last final shaking of the world takes place; there should they be when death overtakes them—doing their duty in that station of life to which God has called them.

Still the men, as they stood, could hold communication with each other, and it soon became known that Mr Charlton had seen an opening some way ahead, through which he believed the ship would pass. To corroborate the truth of this report, he and the master were seen again ascending the rigging. The eyes of both the officers were fixed ahead, or rather over the port-bow. All were now again silent, looking at the captain, and ready to spring at a moment to obey the orders he might give; the second lieutenant and Mr Martin were forward. Mr Charlton made a signal to the captain.

"Up with the helm!—square away the yards!" he shouted.

The order was rapidly executed, and the frigate's head turned towards the dreaded reef; but between the walls of foam an opening of clear water was seen, amply wide to allow her to pass. Almost in an instant, it seemed, she was flying by the danger on an even keel, the breakers sending the spray in heavy showers over her decks. The after-sails were furled: on she flew steadily before the gale. Night came on. There might be other reefs ahead; but the captain and his officers and crew had done all that men could do, and they put their trust in God, who had already brought them safely through so many dangers, that He would protect them.

CHAPTER THIRTEEN

BEN IS SHIPWRECKED

The gale drove the Ajax considerably out of her intended course, and it was some time before she could again haul up to the eastward. It was not without a providential purpose that she was driven in that direction. Three days passed by after the gale had gone down, and just as she had sighted a small island, said to be uninhabited, the look-out at the masthead hailed the deck: "A sail on the lee-bow—five miles away!" he shouted.

Several of the officers went at once aloft, to have a look at the stranger. She was not a large vessel, that was certain; she might be one of the slavers. She must be overhauled at all events; all sail was accordingly made on the frigate. The stranger seemed not to have much wind where she lay; the frigate therefore came rapidly up with her. She was soon seen to be a schooner, and pronounced to have a Spanish look about her. The frigate brought the breeze along with her, and as soon as the schooner felt it, she too made all sail, close-hauled, with an evident intention of escaping. This left little doubt of her character. She was a fast-looking craft, but the Ajax was also noted for her speed, and few on board doubted that the schooner would be overtaken. Everybody was eager to come up with her. What a satisfaction it would be to release the poor savage islanders, and many others of whom they had heard!

The schooner made every effort to escape, and, at last, kept away, finding how fast her pursuer was on a wind, and endeavoured to run back towards the island, her crew probably expecting to be able to escape among the reefs which surrounded it. Fortunately, the island having been well surveyed, a good chart of it existed on board. Captain Bertram was able to stand close in after her without fear. The Ajax came quickly up after the schooner before the wind.

"Try her with a shot, Mr Charlton," said the captain; "but fire high, to injure no one on board."

Mr Sponge, the gunner, with alacrity fired one of the bow chasers. The shot was admirably aimed, and the schooner's maintopmast fell over her side. The frigate's crew uttered a shout of satisfaction.

The slaver, for so she was, did not wait for another, but instantly hauled down her flag. It was that of Chili. The schooner was forthwith hove up in the wind. This done, two boats were seen to leave her side. Captain Bertram, on this, hove the frigate to, and ordered two boats to be manned and to bring the fugitives back, while two others pulled on board the schooner. Ben was in one of the latter, with the interpreter. The crew gave way with a will, for they were eager to get on board. No one was to be seen on deck as they climbed up the sides, but Tatai's hail was at once answered by shouts from below. The hatches were quickly knocked off, and a number of men and women came rushing up, showing, by evident signs, their joy at being liberated. Their first impulse, however, was to fall down on their knees on the deck, and return thanks to Jehovah for having freed them from the barbarians by whom they had been captured. They knew, from having several times before seen the British flag, that they would be kindly treated. They described through Tatai, in pathetic language, the way that they had been treated after having been captured. They had been ordered not to pray aloud, or to sing, and, when off the farther end of this island, to their grief they heard the voices of several of their countrymen, who had come on board. In vain they shouted to warn them. Some at length heard them, and endeavoured to escape. Many sprang overboard into the sea in the hope of swimming on shore, when the inhuman wretches fired on them and killed several; others were knocked down, and, being recaptured, were forced below to join their poor countrymen. This treatment was more than even the patient islanders could stand. By violent efforts, with the aid of a piece of timber they found below, they forced off the hatch and rushed on deck. Some of them threw themselves into the water in the hopes of swimming on shore, though now far from it. At length, the slaver sailed away from the spot, with her cargo of victims to be offered up at the shrine of Mammon; or, in other words, to be destroyed in the silver mines of Peru. Even then, did these till lately savages curse their oppressors? No; even as they sailed away, torn from home and country, wives and children, to die in a foreign land—when they all knelt down at the usual hour to offer up prayer and praise to the God of love and mercy, who had brought them out of darkness into His marvellous light, they did not omit to pray for their cruel oppressors, that their hearts might be converted, and that they might turn to their Maker and live.

Meantime, the boats of the frigate which had gone in chase of the slaver's overtook them, and brought them on board the Ajax. Their guilt was so evident, that Captain Bertram had no doubt about the propriety of detaining them as prisoners. It was necessary, therefore, to send a prize crew to take charge of the schooner. She was called the Andorina (the

Swallow). Mr Owen, the third lieutenant of the frigate, was directed to take charge of the prize, to land the natives at the islands from which they had been taken, and then to follow the frigate to Callao. Mr Manners was to go as his mate. Ben and Tom hoped that they would be among those chosen to form her crew, as boys would certainly be required. Ben wished it, because he should thus be able to make more inquiries for Ned at the places they might touch at, and he made bold to tell his wish to Mr Martin, who suggested it to Mr Charlton. The two boys were therefore delighted when their names were called out to go on board the prize. They quickly mustered with the rest of the prize crew, with their bags ready. The captain addressed them kindly before they left the frigate, urged them to maintain discipline, to obey Mr Owen and Mr Manners, and hoped that he should have a good report of them all when they rejoined the frigate. All arrangements being made, the frigate stood to the eastward with the slaver's crew on board, while the schooner made sail for Samoa, Tonga, and Savage Islands.

The new crew of the schooner had a long voyage before them, but they were in good spirits; they had an abundance of provisions, having been well supplied by the frigate, in addition to what the schooner had before, and they were engaged in a just and humane cause.

It was pleasant to observe the gentle, kind manners of the liberated natives. They were courteous and polite to each other, and they seemed evidently anxious to conform to all the rules and regulations formed for their management. One of them, who had lived some time in the house of a missionary, spoke a little English, and he was thus able to act as interpreter.

Although the crew of the slaver had taken away and thrown overboard one or two Bibles and some other small books, which had been found in the girdles of the captives, they were very far from being deprived of all spiritual comfort, for they could nearly all repeat large portions of the Scripture by heart, many of them entire chapters. They would happily pass many hours of each day repeating these to each other, singing hymns, and offering up prayers. Two or three among them, who were elders of their respective churches, also occasionally addressed and exhorted the rest; indeed, it was a pity that their language was not understood by the white men, who might undoubtedly have learned many an important truth from them. Mr Manners, who was, as has been said, a very sincere Christian, took great interest in their proceedings, and got the young native who spoke English, and who was called Marco, to explain what was said. Ben frequently stood by and listened, and then began to pick up a knowledge of the language.

Thus several days passed by very pleasantly on board the schooner. It has been remarked that this world is a very good and beautiful world, but it is the people who live in it that are bad. In this case the schooner was a very ordinary vessel, and had till lately been filled with very bad people, and a great deal of misery and suffering had existed on board her. Now she was manned with God-fearing and religious people, and so her whole character was changed, and prayers and songs of praise ascended daily from her decks.

The weather, however, was far from satisfactory. The stormy season had set in, and rains and gales of wind might be expected. Mr Owen proved himself a good and careful officer, and, assisted by Mr Manners, was constantly on the watch for the dangers which might befall them. The wind had hitherto been light and contrary, and the schooner had made but little progress. The weather now again became threatening, and caused considerably anxiety to the young officers. It was evident from the look of the sky, and the

W. H. G. Kingston

sudden way in which the sea got up, that another gale was coming on; not so violent, perhaps, as the former, but still requiring every possible preparation to be made for it. The boats and spars, and everything on deck, were doubly secured; the hatches and skylights were fastened down; the topmasts were struck; the lighter sails furled, and storm sails set; and in a short time the schooner was in a state to encounter the expected gale. It came on more gradually than the former one: at first in heavy squalls, and then more and more violently. The sea got up at the same time, and the vessel heeled over to the furious blast Mr Owen and Mr Manners consulted together what course to steer: the schooner could just lie her proper course, and on that course there were no dangers which could not be seen in time, and avoided, as far as they knew. On the other hand, should the gale increase still more, as there was every prospect of its doing, it would be necessary to put her before the wind, as it would be dangerous, if not indeed impossible, to keep her close-hauled as she then was. Should she run for any distance before the gale, she would be carried into a part of the ocean studded thickly with islets. Once among the archipelago, it might be impossible to avoid being dashed on the rock-bound shore of one of them. Here, then, was sufficient cause for anxiety to the young officers. As long as possible, the schooner was kept on a wind, plunging through the seas. Their only other resource was to heave-to; but there was danger in that where neither spars nor rigging could be trusted. The seas came breaking over her bows, and sweeping her decks. Another huge billow, larger and more foam-covered than any of its predecessors, was seen ahead. "Up with the helm, lower the peak, ease away the mainsheet, square away the maintopsail!" cried Mr Owen, with rapid utterance. The crew quickly obeyed his orders. The effect of these orders was to take the pressure off the after-part of the vessel, and round her head flew from the wind and the coming sea. It struck her, however, and from the way it swept along her side, tearing away part of her bulwarks, and doing other damage as it came on board, it was evident that it would have caused far greater disaster had her bow encountered its full force. On she now flew before the hurricane, for such it was rather than a common gale. There was no choice now as to heaving-to. The officers scanned the chart with anxious eyes. They saw, with regret they could scarcely conceal, that, unless the gale should cease, no skill of theirs could save the schooner from destruction, or unless, guided by an unseen Power, she should thread her way amid the labyrinth of islets and reefs ahead of her. Night was coming on. There was no moon. The dark clouds shut out all light from the stars.

On flew the schooner. The unfortunate islanders were invited to come on deck, that, should the vessel strike suddenly, they might have some chance of escaping by swimming on shore. The danger was explained to them through Marco. "We are in the hands of Jehovah," was the answer. "He will do with us what He sees best."

Through the pitchy darkness the vessel rushed on. More than once the quick ears of the seamen detected, they thought, the well-known sound of breakers; but each time the sound died away to leeward: the vessel must have passed at a distance from them. Hour after hour thus passed by. How all on board longed for daylight! Yet daylight would only enable them to see the threatening danger, scarcely to avoid it.

Once more the sound of breakers was heard. This time it was ahead. In vain, with straining eyeballs, the seamen looked into the darkness to discover, if they could, whether the breakers were on the starboard or port bow. All held their breath. The stoutest hearts might then have quailed. The foretopsail was alone set; to have lowered that would have caused the vessel to be pooped, and so more speedily to have sealed her fate. On she flew to destruction. The dreaded crash came. She quivered from stem to stern. Both the masts went by the board, carrying several of the seamen with them, as well as the young commander. Another sea came hissing on astern, threatening to dash the vessel to pieces; but no! it lifted her up, and bore her on its summit far along over the reef.

Mr Manners found himself at that awful moment in command of the schooner. He ordered the well to be sounded. It was not necessary; for the water, it was soon evident, was rushing in through numerous large rents made by the sharp coral. Still the vessel drove on, now among rocks, now in clear water. She was, however, rapidly filling. "Out boats!" was the cry. Fortunately these had escaped injury. Again, however, the schooner was exposed to the fury of the sea, which came sweeping round through a passage in the reef.

At that moment a sudden panic seized the crew. Ben felt himself grasped by the arm, and dragged into one of the boats which had just been lowered. Five men only were in her. Either intentionally or by accident, the painter was let go, and the boat drifted rapidly away from the sinking vessel. The men searched for the oars, which they supposed to be in the boat; only one was to be found. To return to the schooner was therefore impossible. Their only prospect of safety was to get the boat before the wind with the oar. This was done, and farther and farther away she drifted from the vessel.

The men said but little. They regretted being driven away from the schooner without receiving more on board; and Ben heard, with sorrow, that there was but little chance of any of their shipmates being saved. Their own prospects also were gloomy enough. They had no water, no provisions, on board, and one oar alone to guide the boat. One of the most dreadful fates which seamen have sometimes to endure seemed in store for them—to be out on the wide ocean, exposed to the heat of the sun by day and chills by night, without a drop of water to cool their burning thirst. The poor fellows knew too well that this might be their lot; but still they were thankful that they had hitherto escaped the destruction which had overtaken so many of their shipmates.

Two or three of the men at a time were employed in baling out the boat, while one steered as well as he could before the seas. Again the sound of breakers was heard: it was right ahead. "It is all up with us!" cried one of the men. "God be merciful to us!" cried another. Scarcely had they spoken, when the boat was lifted on the foaming summit of a sea, the crest of which nearly filled her with water, and down she came with a crash on the rocks, which dashed her to pieces. Ben clung to one of the fragments. The despairing shrieks of his shipmates sounded in his ears, and he felt himself borne onward into smoother water. He clung tightly to the shattered plank, and thought that he saw trees rising before him. It was not fancy. The dawn had broken, and he was drifting along the shore. He could swim well, and felt sure that he could reach it. A few vigorous strokes, and his feet touched the firm sand. He waded up, and sank exhausted on the dry ground.

The sun was shining brightly on his head before the ship-wrecked lad awoke. He sat up, and, as he recovered his senses, he looked round, hoping to see his companions; but no one was visible. He rose to his feet, and shouted out their names. No reply came to him. He ran along the beach, calling to them; and then discovered that he was on a small island. His voice could, he fancied, have reached from one end to the other. With a sad heart, he found that he was alone—the only human being, as far as he knew, saved from the wreck.

W. H. G. Kingston

CHAPTER FOURTEEN

ON A DESERT ISLAND

Poor Ben was very melancholy at the feeling that he was alone on that desert island; still, he was thankful that his own life had been preserved. "God surely would not have taken me out of the sea to let me die here by inches of hunger and thirst," he said to himself. "I will trust in God, as I have always done." As he said this, he put his hand in the bosom of his shirt. There was safe the little Testament which his mother had given him, and which he had been reading before the gale sprang up. He spread it out open on the sand, that the leaves might dry. "He has spared me this; He has other good things in store for me," he whispered to himself. He also spread out his clothes, which very quickly dried.

Ben had lost his cap, so, while his Testament and clothes were drying, he sat down and began making another out of some broad leaves which grew close at hand. While thus employed, and thinking over what he should do, he recollected that he had not prayed, nor thanked God for preserving him; so, having put on his clothes, he knelt down in the thin shadow of a tall palm, and prayed as he had never prayed before. After doing this, he felt greatly supported; yet his condition was indeed a forlorn one. He rose from his knees, and looked around. He felt thirsty, but not very hungry—sufficiently so, however, to remind him that he must look out for food. He was not aware of the difficulties of procuring it, so that his mind was not troubled on that score. His first idea was to survey the island, so as to learn to a certainty whether any of his shipmates might have been cast on it. He found a piece of timber on the sand, which served him for a walking-stick, and, supported by it, he set off to walk round the island.

He first climbed up to the top of a rock near him, from which, between the trees, he could look across the island, and he thought that it could be little more than half a mile wide. How long it was he could not so well judge. He walked on and on, looking about for signs of fresh-water, for he knew that he must not drink that of the sea. He could find none. He became more and more thirsty; his tongue was parched, and his throat dry: still he would not give up. He dragged his weary feet along, helped by his stick. Some rocky mounds, scarcely to be called hills, appeared in the distance, and he hoped that water might be found near them. This gave him fresh strength to drag himself along. The mounds were not so high even as he had fancied, and were much nearer. Again he was disappointed. He paced round and round them; all was stony and dry.

Ben was very nearly giving way to despair, when he espied, scarcely fifty yards off, a group of tall trees with large round fruit hanging from them. At once he knew them to be cocoa-nuts, and he went on, eager to quench his thirst with the pure milk they contained. Yet, weak as he was, how could he climb up to the top of those trees? He had often seen the natives do it with a band round their waists. If he were strong, he might do it in the same way, could he but find the band; but, in his weak state, that was impossible. Again he was doomed to disappointment, he feared, and was about to pursue his exploring tour, when he saw, not far off, a nut on the ground. He ran eagerly and picked it up. It had been blown off during the recent gale. After stripping off the husk, he soon broke in the end; and, though he spilt a little, there was sufficient milk in it to quench his now burning thirst. He then more slowly ate pieces of the fruit, which he cut out with his knife. Here was one means of supporting life, and Ben's elastic spirits again rose. At his age the thoughts of the future did not press heavily on him. He had, too, 'a conscience void of offence towards God': not that he did not feel and know himself to be a sinner; but he felt himself to be a pardoned one, as a sincere believer in Christ. That was the secret of his light-heartedness. Still he had a longing for pure water. He knew, too, that he could the better cook any fish he might obtain if he could find it. How was he to light a fire, however? Just before the gale came on, the cook had sent him below to get his tin-box of matches, and after the cook had taken one out, Ben had put it into his pocket. There it was, and, the lid fitting tightly down, the matches were uninjured. "I must cherish them carefully, however," he thought; "when they are gone, I shall be unable to light a fire." He looked about and found several other cocoa-nuts, which he collected, and piled up where he could again find them.

Much refreshed, Ben continued his walk. At last he saw the end of the island. For a quarter of a mile or more it was low and barren, hard rock washed apparently by the sea; so he turned round and went back by the other shore. The island was, altogether, nearly two miles long; but there were not many cocoa-nut trees on it,—nor much soil indeed, which was the reason probably that it was not inhabited. He might now exclaim, though sadly, "I am monarch of all I survey;" but he would rather have been the meanest subject of a small kingdom, with civilised companions, than a king and all alone on that nearly barren reef. Still he had no fear of starving; shell-fish he saw on the rocks in abundance. During the calm, too, some of the natives had been fishing over the side of the vessel, and he also had got some hooks and a long line. These he had put into his pockets. He might, he hoped, find some roots, and thus be able to vary his diet. As the sun rose, the horizon became very clear, and he thought that he could distinguish land in one direction; it was at all events a long way off, and it was so faint that it might be only a cloud just rising above the horizon. He should be able to judge better after watching it for a day or two.

As Ben walked on, his eye was continually roving about for signs of water. How gladly would he have welcomed the sight of even a little mossy pool, or some moisture in the crevice of a rock! He did not despair. He had hitherto only explored the shore; water might rise in the interior, and be lost in the sand before it reached the beach. "One thing I ought to have before night," he said,—for he had got into the way of talking aloud,—"that is, shelter. I must build myself a hut;" and so he set to work. There were canes, and bushes, and broad leaves of the pandanus and other trees in abundance. He did not require a very spacious mansion; still he wanted one high enough to sit in. He worked on till he was tired and hungry. He had left his cocoa-nuts some way off, and had to go for them. He brought as many as he could carry back to his hut. Knocking a hole in the end of one of them, and carefully scraping out the fruit after he had drunk the milk, he waded into the water, and cut some mussels off the rocks. His cocoa-nut he filled with salt-water. Coming back, he lighted a fire in a hole a little way from his hut. Would he put his cocoa-nut on it? No; he was too wise for that; but he made some stones red-hot, and kept tumbling them into the water till the mussels were sufficiently cooked. Others he toasted before the fire, but he liked the boiled ones best. He thus made a tolerably substantial meal. To keep in his fire, he built up a wall of stones round it, and put on a quantity of green sticks, which would burn slowly, hoping in that way to save the expenditure of another match.

"I will finish my hut, and then I will go and have another hunt for water," he said to himself, as he began working again. He had placed his hut against a tree, with the opening turned away from the wind. There were plenty of dry leaves about, which he collected for his bed. He did not require furniture; that he would make by and by. While hunting in his pockets for the matches, he found a number of thin flat seeds. He recollected having saved them from a fruit of the gourd species, which had been used on board the schooner. He carefully dried them and put them by, remembering that such things grow very rapidly. "There will be no harm sowing them; if I do not use them, others will. I am thankful I found them," he thought. Once more he set out to look for water. The exertion he had gone through, and the heat, made the milk of the cocoa-nut insufficient for quenching his thirst. The ground was rough; but he eagerly clambered over it, backwards and forwards, hoping thus to find a spring if one existed. The sun was sinking low, when he thought that the trees and shrubs, in a hollow he saw some way before him, looked greener and more luxuriant than those in other places. "Water makes leaves and grass green," he said to himself; "I hope so, for I don't think that I could live many more hours without water, not through another day in this hot sun. Oh dear! oh dear! how very, very thirsty I am! What would I give if there should be water there, even though I should only get one good drink of it! Ay, but I shall want it another day—for many days, or months, perhaps, as long as I live on this island. I don't think that God will have put only a little there. If there is any, there will be a good supply for me, more than this cocoa-nut full, I am certain." He had brought a cocoa-nut shell with him to fill with water, that he might take some back to his hut.

Ben almost shouted for joy when he found a spring of pure

water bubbling up from under a big rock. It ran a little way between rocks, and then lost itself in a sandy bed. He scooped a hole in the ground, into which he put his cocoa-nut shell, which quickly filled with water. How sweet and pure it tasted! He felt that he could never take enough. At last, however, his thirst was quenched, so he filled his cocoa-nut shell, and directed his steps to the sea-shore; but he had not gone far before he was tempted to put the shell to his lips. He soon drained it, and then he went back for more. His great fear was that he should not again find the spring. He marked the spot with the greatest care, and noted each tree and mound as he took his way towards the beach. Night was coming on, as it does in those latitudes, very rapidly; and Ben had to hurry on for fear of not finding his hut, and at the same time to be very cautious not to spill the water out of his cocoa-nut. Oh that people would be as eager for the Water of Life, as little Ben was for the spring in that desert island, and would be tempted to return to it again and again to drink afresh of its pure source! Ben was thankful when he saw the glow from his fire, which continued smouldering gently. Without it he might have passed his hut. He could not manage by its light to read more than a few verses from his Testament; but even those few gave him comfort and hope. With a heart truly grateful for the mercies bestowed on him, he knelt down and offered up his simple prayer to God. The last thing he did was to make up his fire afresh, and then he crept into his hut and in a few moments was fast asleep.

The sun had risen before Ben awoke. He felt that he had a great deal to do. He could not tell how long he might have to remain on the island. It might be not only for months, but for years. Much depended on his own sense and energy whether he would retain his health, or indeed life itself. He began the day with prayer and reading the Testament. He knew that that was the best way at all events to save himself from turning into a savage. He then made his breakfast off cocoa-nut and shell-fish. "I must catch some fish, however," he said to himself, as he finished the last clam; "this food will not do to live on always. I may find some roots and berries, and perhaps turtles' eggs. I heard some wild-fowl cry last evening; I may find their eggs too, and trap them or some other birds, or get a turtle itself. The first thing I'll now do is to carry my hut nearer to the water, instead of having to bring the water all this way to the hut. That won't take long. I can carry the whole of it in two journeys, and quickly put it up. I must take the fire after it. That will keep in for many hours, I see, with the help of this rotten wood. If I go working on in these clothes, I shall soon wear them out. I must see what I can do to make others out of the bark of the paper-mulberry, as the natives do; I thought I saw some of those trees yesterday. I daresay I shall not succeed at first, but there is nothing like trying. There is a piece of open ground near the spring which will just do for the gourd-seeds. I'll sow them therein forthwith. The fruit is very wholesome, I know; and the dried gourds will furnish me with basins and pots and pans in abundance."

Ben put all his plans into execution in a methodical, regular way. He became, indeed, perfectly happy, and almost cont-ented with his lot, except when he thought of his mother and Ned—poor Ned, still undiscovered, living among savages, or on a desert island, like himself. His own fate made him hope more than ever that Ned had escaped.

Now and then the course of his plans was interrupted by something else which occurred to him to do. One idea was to erect a beacon at each end of the island, to attract the attention of those on board any passing vessel. He had nothing of which to make a flag, so a flagstaff would have been of no use. It then struck him that a cross would be more remarkable than anything else, and he devoted a part of each day to the work. It was a very heavy task. He chose a tree towards the end of the island, where he proposed erecting the first cross. He had only a stout pocket-knife, but he could employ fire, and that only required constant watching. A large sharp stone helped him. When he had thus felled the tree, he had to cut off the branches, and to drag it to the end of the island. With great labour he partly burned, and partly cut, a deep notch, into which he fixed the cross-beam, securing it with wedges. He had observed a cleft in the rock: in this he placed the butt-end, and gradually raised it with far more ease than he could otherwise have done. Some large stones placed round it kept it secure. The other cross was erected much in the same manner.

His fishing was very successful, and he was soon able to catch an ample supply for his daily food. He found, too, some roots which were perfectly wholesome. When cultivated by the natives, they formed one of their chief articles of food. He was not disappointed in finding, after a time, some turtles' and sea-fowls' eggs; indeed, he had an abundance of nutritious food, gained, however, by his own exertions and perseverance. It might have been possible for a person to have died of starvation on the island, simply on account of not looking for the means of subsistence which it afforded. Ben not only collected for present use, but preserved what he could for the future, knowing that at certain seasons the turtle and wild-fowl would cease to lay eggs, that the fish might leave the coast, or that stormy weather might prevent his catching them; that the cocoa-nuts would dry up, as might the roots, and that the wild-fowl might become more wary. He was thus never idle, from morning till night; and though, of course, he thought very often of home and Ned, and of how he should get away, yet he never was unhappy or out of spirits. He was as fond as ever of saying, "Do right, whatever comes of it, and trust in God."

W. H. G. Kingston

CHAPTER FIFTEEN

ESCAPE: AND THE END OF BEN'S HISTORY

Ben had recollected the day of the week on which, he was cast on the island. By means of a stick which he notched regularly, a plan he had often heard of being adopted under similar circumstances, he kept an exact note of the days as they passed. Sunday he made a day of rest. It was not, however, a day of weariness. He read much more than usual of his Testament, and, recollecting the way the natives had repeated portions of it, he set to work to commit some of its chapters to memory.

This he found a delightful occupation. When doing so, he spent many hours walking up and down on the smooth sea sand, with shoeless feet, looking out every now and then on the blue ocean, and thinking what a beautiful world it is we inhabit, and how grievous that man should mar it by his evil temper and wicked deeds. Then he would occasionally sing all the hymns he knew at the top of his voice, from very joyfulness of heart. In the week-days, when at work, he would repeat over what he had learned on the Sundays. Thus five months, by his calculation, passed away.

One Monday forenoon, as he was going out to the end of a reef to fish, on looking in the direction where he had frequently seen what he supposed to be land, he saw an object moving over the water. It was not white, like the sail of a vessel. It must, then, be the mat-sail of a large double canoe. Thinking no more of his fishing, he ran up to the highest rocky hill in the neighbourhood to watch its progress. It was drawing nearer the island, and yet apparently not steering directly for it, rather, as it were, to pass at some distance.

"I wonder what sort of people are on board," he thought. "Perhaps savages—cannibals. Then it will be much better if they do not come here. If they are Christian natives, then I shall be very glad to go with them, as they of course are on their way to some civilised island where ships are likely to call."

The wind was light, the canoe moved slowly, and Ben's anxiety increased. At last it seemed clear that the canoe would not come nearer to the island. He heaved a deep sigh, and sat silent and sad for some time. Then he recollected that he was going to fish. He got up, and again worked his way towards the end of the reef. He cast in his line, and had hooked a fish, when, just as he landed it, on looking up for an instant, he saw the canoe gliding towards the island. It was steering for the point on which stood the cross, there could be no doubt about that. He watched it eagerly, anxious to ascertain who was on board. If they were savages, should he hide himself, and trust to their going away again? "Yet even if they are savages, they will not hurt me," he said to himself. "They will see at once that I cannot do them any harm. I will run and meet them, and welcome them. That will be the best way, I am sure. I will take a branch in my hand, and wave it as the natives do, to show that I wish to be friendly with them."

Saying this, Ben drew up the fish he had hooked,—a fine

W. H. G. Kingston

large one,—retreated along the reef over the rocks, cut a branch, and ran along the beach as fast as his legs could carry him towards Cross Point. He got there before the canoe, for the wind was light. He could see a number of people on it as it drew nearer. Were they savages? They were all clothed. Yes, and some of them were dressed as English sailors. There was a glitter of gold-lace on the coat of one of them. In the bow stood a young sailor lad. Gradually the faces began to grow distinct. How his heart leaped with joy! There were Tom Martin and Mr Manners, and several of the prize crew he had long thought in their ocean graves, and there were also a good number of the natives, busy in lowering the huge mat-sail of the canoe. They were the very men who had been on board the schooner.

Ben was at first almost beside himself with delight. He waved his hands and shouted wildly; then he ran down and showed them the best place for bringing the canoe to shore. The natives cried out to him, but neither Tom Martin nor any of the English seamen seemed to know him. "I wonder what that little savage wants," he heard Tom say to one of the men. "He looks to me as if he was out of his senses."

"No, I am not, Tom Martin, I can assure you," cried Ben, running up to him and putting out his hand; "only very, very glad to see you again, and to find that you are all alive."

"Well, indeed, I am also glad to find you were not drowned, Ben," answered Tom, wringing his shipmate's hand till it seemed as if he would wring it off. "I felt certain that you were drowned, and was very sorry for you, that I was!"

"He speaks truth, Ben," observed Jem Stokes, a seaman who had always stood Tom's friend. "The lad took so ill when he thought that you were lost, that we thought he would have slipped his cable altogether; but Mr Manners spoke to him, as he did to all of us, and told him that if you had left this world you had gone to a better."

Jem's remarks were cut short by Mr Manners, who had now come on shore. Ben was not aware, till he observed the surprised look with which his officer regarded him, of the odd figure he cut. He then recollected that he wore a suit of his own home-made clothes: a hat of leaves, in shape between an extinguisher and an umbrella; a cape of mulberry-tree cloth, and a kilt of the same, reaching down to his knees. With shoes he had learned to dispense, that he might have a good pair to go away in. He had worn them, however, on Sunday mornings, when he had put them on, with the rest of his best suit. Ben explained to Mr Manners why he was dressed in that curious fashion, and the young officer highly approved of his reasons, and complimented him on his ingenuity in their manufacture.

The whole party then collected round him while he gave a brief account of the way he had been preserved, and how he had managed to subsist during his sojourn on the island. He, in return, was informed how his friends had escaped. The schooner, from having no cargo in her, did not sink as soon as was expected, but drove on to another reef, where she stuck fast. The gale falling soon after, those on board had time to construct a raft, on which, with the aid of one of the boats, they reached an island which they had seen five or six miles off. They were able to save a small quantity of provisions; but the larger portion, being under water, could not be got at. The island was of considerable size, and, thanks to the knowledge possessed by the natives, they had not experienced much difficulty in procuring food. The schooner soon broke up, so that very little more was got out of her, and only a few articles of value were washed ashore. Mr Manners at once proposed building a vessel; but the carpenter's mate, who had come in the schooner as carpenter, had been lost when the vessel went on the rocks, and none of the other men knew anything of ship-building. The natives, on hearing the wish of the English officer, offered to construct a large double canoe, three or four professional canoe-builders being among them. They were far more ingenious than the civilised Englishmen. Their tools they made out of stones, and flints, and shells; the fibre of trees served them instead of nails; their sails were made out of dried grass. It was a work, however, of great labour; night and day they toiled at it. At length, aided by the Englishmen, it was completed. They had preserved and stored all the food they could collect and spare for their voyage; but their great difficulty was to carry enough water. The water on the island was bad, and they had not sufficient receptacles for it. Still, they hoped to reach some island where they might replenish their stock; but that was very uncertain.

"Indeed, the possibility—or, I may say, the probability—of our running short of water is the greatest cause of anxiety I have for our dangerous voyage. If that was over, I should have fewer cares on my mind," observed Mr Manners.

"Then, sir, I think that I can certainly relieve you of that care," answered Ben. "There is a spring of excellent water in the middle of the island, and near it I planted, on the second day of my arrival, some gourd-seeds. The plants grew up very fast, and the fruit has now become of great size, and is perfectly ripe. Each of them would, I should think, when dried, hold a large quantity of water; and I am sure that the pulp is very good and wholesome, for I have felt much better since I lived on it. Besides, I have already dried a number of the outsides, so that we may judge how they hold water."

"That is indeed providential, Ben," observed Mr Manners. "God, I believe, never allows anything to be done without an object; and it seems very clear that you were thrown on this island, not only that your own life might be saved, but that you might be the means of preserving all our lives. Had it not been for you, we should not have known that there exists water on the island; and we certainly should not have had the means of carrying it away. Let us at once examine the gourds, that we may see what can be done."

Mr Manners now called Marco, and begged him to set off at once with Ben, and examine the gourds, with a few of the other natives, while the rest dispersed on the island to collect roots, cocoa-nuts, and, indeed, any other food that they could find.

Ben could not help feeling proud at the commendation which Mr Manners bestowed on his hut and its internal arrangements; still more so on his plantation of gourds. The little seeds which he had brought to shore in his jacket-pocket had now become large plants, producing gourds twice the size of a man's head. As he had wisely planted them at a distance from each other, they had all grown to their full size. Marco selected thirty, at least, each of which would hold several quarts of water; while their pulp was a welcome addition to the food of those who had been for so long living on the produce of the sea, and roots, and cocoa-nuts.

Three days were spent in drying the gourds and in filling them, and in replenishing the other receptacles on board the canoe with the pure water from Ben's fountain. One or two defects in the canoe were also made good, and a considerable addition to their supply of provisions was taken on board.

Ben took a last look at the hut he had so long inhabited, and the garden he had cultivated with so much care, with a feeling almost of regret, knowing that he was to part from them for ever. Before leaving them, however, he planted a number of ripe seeds, and repaired his hut, in case any other person might be cast on shore on the island. The crosses were also repaired.

"We had not intended landing on the island till we saw them," observed Mr Manners. "When our eyes caught sight of them, we knew that some Christian person must be, or must have been, on the island; and, though eager to proceed on our voyage, we at once resolved to touch at the place. I pray that, before long, the time may come for the cross to be erected on every island throughout the wide Pacific, not as the symbol of nominal Christianity, of a religion of forms and ceremonies, but as the sign of a true and living faith, of a spiritual worship acceptable to God."

The last remarks, though spoken aloud, were made by Mr Manners rather to himself than to those near him.

All preparations having been made, the whole party, with Ben Hadden, embarked on board the canoe. She was paddled out into the open sea, the wind was fair, the sail was hoisted, and Ben soon saw his island home sink beneath the horizon.

The difficulties in the navigation of the voyage just commenced were very great. Mr Manners had saved only a boat's compass; he had no quadrant and no chart. He calculated that they were about sixteen hundred miles at least from Samoa, for which group he shaped his course. They expected to meet with several islands on the way, but though the inhabitants of some of them had been converted to Christianity, those of others were still sunk in heathen darkness and barbarism. It would be necessary for them, therefore, to be very careful on which they landed. In the one case, they would be sure of a friendly reception; in the other they would be attacked, and probably murdered, if not on their guard. Ben hoped that at all events they might touch at several islands, that he might have more opportunities of making inquiries about Ned. He found that strict discipline was maintained on board the canoe. All on board were divided into watches, taking regularly their turns of duty. Morning and evening there were prayers, led by Mr Manners in English and by Marco in his own language. The day was begun by all joining in a hymn, then the Scriptures were read and commented on by the respective readers. Ben was very glad to find that Tom took a great interest in their services, and spoke on religious subjects in a tone that he had never before done.

"Why, you see, Ben," said Tom, "on that awful night of the wreck I thought that we were all going to be drowned, and when, after all, we got on shore, I felt how merciful and kind God had been to save such a wicked fellow as I was, instead of you, who was so much more fit to go to Him. I was still very sorry for you, for your mother's sake, and I knew father would be very sorry when he heard of it. I do not suppose that those thoughts would have lasted very long; I am afraid not: but then, Mr Manners spoke to me so kindly, that I felt what an ungrateful wretch I should be if I didn't give my heart to so good and merciful a God; and from that day to this I have been trying to do so. It is not very easy, even among the few of our poor fellows remaining; but Mr Manners says that I must pray for grace, and not trust to my own strength, and that then, if I am sincere and not a hypocrite to myself, that I should have every confidence of being supported and protected. It is that thought, Ben, which gives me so much comfort. Otherwise I should be very unhappy, and not at all sure that I should not be a castaway after all."

"That is just the same thought that has made me always happy," remarked Ben. "I know that God never casts out any who go to Him through Christ, and trust to Him completely, and not to themselves, while they try to love and serve Him

W. H. G. Kingston

as much as they can, though that is very little after all I can't tell you, though, Tom, how glad I am to hear you speak so, and I am sure that your father will be still more glad, if we ever find the ship again, which I hope we may do."

"That's the very thing I am afraid of," said Tom. "I shall be very glad indeed to see my father again; but when I get back among the other boys, and into old ways again, I shall be apt to do just as before, and to talk nonsense and play all my old tricks. I say, Ben, if we ever do get back, you must help me! Won't you, there's a good fellow?"

Of course Ben promised Tom that he would help him as much as he could, though he reminded him also that he must depend on himself in one sense, though not on his own strength, for that effectual strength he could alone obtain through the aid of the Holy Spirit.

The wind was light, and the sea calm, and the canoe glided smoothly over the water. She was of a curious construction, being in reality two canoes connected by a very strong platform. The mast was a triangle, which supported a mat-sail spread on a long yard. The vessel had not to go about; but, as the stem and stern were alike, she sailed equally well both ways. At each end there were long oars, which served as rudders; but in calms she was impelled by paddles, and could thus also be moved at a considerable rate. Nobody on board was idle. In calm weather every one was employed in paddling or steering. Mr Manners took his turn with the rest. If there was a sea,—that is to say, if it was rough,—Ben and Tom, with the assistance of two or three others, had enough to do to bale out the water. A constant look-out was also necessary, to avoid any reefs or low islands in their course. Ben was very happy. He had been so long without talking, that it was a satisfaction to him once more to use his tongue, though still greater to hear other people talk, especially Mr

Manners and Tom, when they spoke on subjects in which he was interested. As for his own tongue, when once set going, he found no little difficulty in again stopping it.

The weather continued so calm, that it was impossible to say to what extent the voyage might be prolonged: it was necessary, therefore, to use the greatest economy in the consumption of water and their scanty supply of provisions. A small allowance of food and water was served out to each person three times a day; but no one grumbled, for all saw the necessity of the arrangement.

Six days had passed by since the canoe had left Ben Hadden's island, as Mr Manners called it, when land was sighted ahead, or rather, the trees which grew on it, for their tops were first seen. It was an island extending for three or four miles across the horizon. No one on board knew anything about the island, but they hoped that they might there obtain a fresh supply of water and provisions, and, should it be inhabited by Christians, that they might gain some information as to their direct course for Samoa. Accordingly they steered for an opening which appeared in the barrier-reef. On getting through it, other rocks were seen ahead, and Mr Manners was afraid, should he stand on, of injuring the canoe. The sail was lowered, and they were about to paddle off again in order to search for a safe landing-place, when a man was seen on the shore beckoning them. First he pointed to the right hand, by which they knew that they were to sail in that direction; then he beckoned directly to himself, afterwards to the left, and so on. By following his directions, they reached the beach in safety. He was a wild-looking person dressed in a leaf hat, something like the one Ben had made for himself, with a seaman's tattered jacket, and a kilt of native cloth. His feet and legs were bare, his hair was long, and hung down over his shoulders, while in his hand he carried a heavy club, which

W. H. G. Kingston

he grasped tightly, as if he considered it likely to prove a friend in need. Notwithstanding his wild appearance, it was easy to perceive by the colour of his skin, sunburnt as it was, that he was not a native. He seemed very much surprised at seeing white men on board the canoe, for he did not appear to have discovered that till they were on the point of landing. He did not, however, address them, but spoke to the natives in a language which they understood. Marco inquired of him whether there were other inhabitants on the island, and whether they were Christians. He said that there were a great many; that they were not *Lota*, that is Christians, but that they were a very good sort of people. They had sent him on to the end of the reef to pilot in the canoe, he said, and they themselves would soon come to welcome the strangers. He had scarcely spoken before a large number of wild, nearly naked savages came out from among the trees. They were armed with spears and clubs, had long matted hair like a black thatch over their heads, and were altogether a very forbidding, unattractive set of beings. Still, from what they said to Marco and the other natives, and by their actions, they appeared to be friendlily disposed towards their visitors. It was near evening, and they signified that, if the visitors would remain overnight, they would the next day bring all the provisions required, and plenty of calabashes of pure water, which they stated was to be obtained in the middle of the island. Mr Manners thanked them, and said that he would remain till the next day. The natives then invited them to come and sleep on shore; but this Mr Manners declined, as he preferred sleeping on board the canoe. To allow more room on board, he said that he would not object to some of his people building huts of boughs for themselves on the beach, but urged them on no account to go to a distance from it. The natives, however, to show their good intentions, brought down to the beach a supply of taro and other roots and fruits, likewise as much fresh-water as their visitors would require. They seemed, as Mr Manners thought, rather disappointed that no one would accompany them away from the shore. They stood by while the provisions were being cooked, rather astonished at the proceeding; still greater was their surprise when the natives sung a hymn and offered up a prayer before they began to eat. What it could all mean of course they could not tell, but they probably had an idea that it was some sort of incantation, for they were seen to draw back for some distance, and not till the hymn was finished did they return, when they stood looking on as before.

Ben and Tom, with two of the English seamen, were allowed to go on shore that they might draw the white man, if possible, into conversation, if he could speak English. He had hitherto kept aloof from the strangers, and even stood behind his native companions while the hymn was being sung. When the natives had finished singing, Ben stood up and said the short grace which his father had been accustomed to repeat before meals. The white man, who at that time was standing a little way apart from his companions while Ben was speaking, drew nearer to him, and seemed to be listening attentively.

"I say, old fellow, come and have something to eat," said one of the seamen, holding out a bit of taro at the end of his knife.

The white man looked wistfully towards the strangers; then he cast a glance at the scowling, savage-looking natives who were watching him, and, shaking his head, again drew farther back from them. There he sat without speaking, and each time either Ben or Tom, or the other two seamen, addressed him, he shook his head, as if either he did not understand, or, at all events, did not wish to hold any communication with them.

While the party who purposed sleeping on the shore were

putting up their huts, and collecting leaves for their beds, the natives and the white man, as before, stood watching them, but made no offer of assistance. The Christian visitors again sang a hymn, as the sun set and darkness came on. Then commending themselves to the protection of Heaven, they crept into their huts, and lay down to sleep. Ben and his shipmates, finding that the natives and their white associate had gone away, soon after followed their example; one of the seamen promising to sleep with one eye open, so as to be on the watch, though it was the opinion of all that the natives were a quiet sort of people, who would do them no harm. There was no moon; but the sky was clear, and the bright stars which glittered forth from it in countless numbers, in that pure atmosphere, afforded sufficient light to enable objects to be visible at a little distance.

Ben had slept for some time, he fancied, when he was awakened by feeling a hand placed on his arm.

"Hist, youngster! don't lie sleeping there," whispered a voice in his ear. "Rouse up the other Englishmen. Get on board the canoe, and be off, or you'll all be murdered. Never mind the natives with you. If you wake them up, there'll be a noise, and the people of the place will be down on them. Don't speak above a whisper, whatever you do. The people are not far off, and I found it a hard job to steal away."

Ben at once comprehended that some danger was threatened. He sat up, and saw the stranger white man standing over him.

"Leave our Christian friends! No, we will never do that," he answered. "I will go and arouse them, while you can awake my shipmates; and, whoever you are, you must come with us."

"Well, well, I'll do as you wish," answered the white man; "only be sharp, and tell the people to creep along over the ground, so as not to be seen at a distance. We must climb into the canoe, and shove off without any noise, or they will be down on us before we can get clear of the reefs."

Without wasting more time on words, Ben crept off to where Marco was sleeping; he had fortunately noted the place. Awaking him, he told him of the warning he had received, and Marco quickly aroused the rest of his party.

It was with difficulty that the seamen could be prevented from speaking when called; in a couple of minutes, however, the whole party were creeping down towards the canoe, which lay afloat alongside some rocks running into the water. They were all quickly on board, followed by the young Englishman—for such it was supposed the white man was, by his language.

"Shove off, sir!" he whispered to Mr Manners, who had only then been aroused. "No time to lose. I will go to the helm."

The advice was instantly followed; the warps were cast off, the paddles got out, and the canoe began slowly to glide out from among the rocks. Scarcely, however, had she begun to move than loud shouts were heard, and large numbers of the savage natives were seen rushing down from among the trees to the beach. When they found that the canoe had moved from the rocks, they yelled and shouted more fiercely than ever.

"Give way, lads! give way!" cried the stranger; "there is a narrow place where they may catch us if we are not smart."

Neither the English seamen nor the natives required any urging, but paddled away as hard as they could. They saw

W. H. G. Kingston

the savages indeed, their figures standing out against the sky, as they hurried along over the rocks, shouting, and leaping, and brandishing their spears. Before the canoe had got far, a shower of spears and darts fell among the party on board; but, thrown from a distance, not much injury was done, and they were only stimulated to increased exertion. Alone, they could not, in the dark, have found their way out through the passage in the reefs; the young man, however, seemed confident that he knew the right course to steer. Not a word was spoken; each man paddled as hard as he could. Gradually the rocks were left behind, and the last passage between the reefs was seen; beyond was the open sea. The shouts and shrieks of the savages became fainter and fainter. They either had not had time to launch their canoes, or were afraid to attack the large double canoe in them. In a short time Mr Manners and his companions were in safety.

Once more a course was steered for Samoa. All were thankful for their narrow and providential escape, and did not fail to express their gratitude to the young Englishman who had been the means of preserving their lives. He, however, seemed unwilling to talk on the subject.

"Nothing particular, sir, to thank me for," he answered. "Less said about it the better, according to my notion."

It was fortunate that they had economised their small stock of water and provisions, as they had been unable to replenish them at the island from which they had just escaped. It was necessary to be even still more careful than before, because it might be some time before they could reach any other island where they could obtain what they required.

Most of the English seamen were loud in their threats of vengeance against the savages, for their treacherous conduct.

"If we ever reach the old Ajax, we would like to get her to go back and blow the fellows to pieces," said one.

"No, no; that is not the way to treat them," observed Marco, when he understood what was said. "The way to treat them will be to send a missionary to teach them better things. With God's aid, that will we do as soon as we reach our own island, or can let our brethren at Raratonga know of their condition."

"Yes, you do speak like a real Christian, Marco," answered the seaman who had thoughtlessly made the proposal. "That's the right way, to be sure: I didn't mean that I would really wish to kill the poor savages, for of course they don't know better."

The next morning the wind was fair, the sea smooth, and the canoe glided swiftly over the waters. The work of the day was commenced, as usual, with a hymn and a prayer, and then the Scriptures were read. The young stranger stood aloof, disinclined, as it seemed, to join in the service. At length, Mr Manners invited him to join in the prayer he was about to offer up with his own men in English.

"Thank ye, sir," answered the stranger, giving the usual seaman's pull at his hair, when addressing an officer. "It's so long since I have prayed, that I have forgotten how."

"That is a sad thing, my lad," answered Mr Manners, "the sooner, then, you begin the better. Did you ever learn how to read your Bible?"

"Once, sir, long ago; but I have forgotten all about that too, I am afraid," answered the stranger. "For better than three years I haven't spoken a word of English. I don't think I could read, even if I was to try ever so much."

"We will see about that after we have had prayers," said Mr Manners in a kind tone. "There is a lad here who never, I believe, misses reading the Bible every day of his life, if he can avoid it. He will help me to teach you; won't you, Ben?"

"Yes, sir, very gladly," said Ben Hadden, who was appealed to.

After prayers, and when Mr Manners had offered up thanks for the preservation of himself and his companions from the hands of the treacherous savages, Ben brought out his well-worn Testament, which was somewhat the worse for the wetting it had got in salt-water, and, at a sign from Mr Manners, he went up to the stranger, and offered to read to him. Mr Manners told him to select the parable of the Prodigal Son, and several other portions of Scripture likely to interest a person whose mind had long been dormant to spiritual matters. The young man was evidently very much interested. Suddenly he interrupted Ben by remarking—

"That's just such a book as I once had. I remember it well. My father gave it to me just before I went to sea. I lost it, though, and have never looked into another since."

"My father gave this to me, and I've kept it carefully ever since. I wouldn't lose it for worlds," said Ben. "Look here: he wrote my name in it with his own hand. See: 'Benjamin Hadden'—though I was always called in our parts, Little Ben Hadden."

"You Ben Hadden!" exclaimed the stranger in a husky voice. "Did you ever hear speak of your brother Ned?"

"Yes indeed," cried Ben eagerly; "I came out to these parts to look for him. Can you tell me anything about him?"

"Well, I should think so," answered the stranger in the same husky voice as before; "though, to be sure, I cannot tell you much in his favour. What should you say if I was to tell you that I am Ned Hadden?"

"You my brother Ned!" exclaimed Ben, in a half-disappointed and doubting tone of voice. "You wouldn't deceive me, surely. I have long and long wished to find him. But are you indeed my brother Ned? Oh, tell me! tell me!"

"Yes, I am Ned Hadden—or was, there is no doubt about that; but I have become such a savage sort of chap, that I don't know very well what I am now."

Ben seized Ned's hand, and burst into tears. His brother was so different from what he had expected to find him—so rough and savage-looking almost, and ignorant; yet he was thankful that he had found him. Afterwards, when he thought the matter over, he saw that he had still greater reason to be thankful that he had found him, for Ned's own sake: the more savage and ignorant he was, the more important that he should be instructed in the truths of the gospel. From that moment forward that was Ben's daily, hourly task. He wished the voyage to be prolonged, that he might have his brother more to himself, to read to him, and teach him the Truth. Mr Manners took great pleasure in helping him in his pious task, and it was easy to see that Ned profited greatly by their instruction. His first inquiries had been for his family. He was much affected by hearing of the death of his father and brothers. That very event seemed to soften his heart, and make him willing to listen attentively to what Mr Manners and Ben said to him. He confessed that, when the canoe was seen approaching the island, he had consented to assist the natives in decoying her in, with the intention of destroying all on board; but that, on hearing the hymn sung, and, more than all, on listening to Ben's grace, the words of which sounded familiar to his ears, recollecting his early principles, he resolved to save the visitors, whom he also knew to be his countrymen.

All this came out but slowly, as his mind expanded under the instruction he was receiving. He had been so long among savages and heathens that he had imbibed many of their notions and principles; instead of improving them, he had nearly sunk to their level. Such has unhappily been the case with numerous European and American sailors, who have either been wrecked or have deserted their ships, and have lived long among the once savage inhabitants of the islands of the Pacific. Many of them have proved, by their evil influence and example, sad hindrances to the efforts of the missionaries in spreading among the natives the truths of the gospel.

For several days the canoe glided slowly on. Though strongly built, her form was not equal to those constructed by the Tonga islanders, noted for their speed among the surrounding groups of islands.

Mr Manners had begun to grow very anxious with regard to their provisions and water. Before he could hope to reach their final destination, it would be absolutely necessary to touch at some island where they might replenish their stock, both of one and the other. The weather, too, had shown signs of changing; and the sea, hitherto so calm, began to tumble and toss the canoe about in a way which strained her greatly, and made it necessary for a number of those on board to be continually baling. As the sea increased more and more, it was necessary to do this night and day without ceasing. All on board were accordingly looking out anxiously for some island where they might find shelter till the stormy weather was over.

For two days the wind had been increasing, and when night came on it was already blowing a heavy gale. The sail was lowered, and the canoe drove before it, kept by the rudder and paddles from broaching to. The night became very dark; on drove the canoe; breakers were heard not far off, and most of those on board believed that their last hour was come.

Presently the canoe was among the breakers, and the sea swept over her deck. Her crew with difficulty held on. In another moment she struck, and it seemed certain that she would be dashed to atoms. Still she floated, and the water became less broken. She drove on; her bow struck violently on a sandy beach, and tall trees rose before the eyes of those on board. They rushed forward, and as the wave receded they scrambled upwards till they reached the dry sand. How could they tell, though, that they were not to meet with the fate from which they had a few days before escaped? The lives of all were mercifully preserved, but it seemed too likely that their canoe had suffered some material injury from the blows she had received. A few, not without risk, ventured again on board, and succeeded in landing most of their scanty supply of provisions and water. A fire was then, after some time, lighted, round which they collected to dry their drenched garments.

They were all too anxious to sleep. Soon after daybreak, some persons were seen approaching in the distance. "Good news, my friends," exclaimed Marco, who was watching them; "they wear the dress of Christians; they are clothed and in their right mind." A party of natives now came up, and cordially welcomed the shipwrecked strangers. Some hurried back to bring water and provisions, others examined the canoe, which it was pretty evident was not in a condition again to go to sea. Marco found that he could very easily understand them; so could also Ned Hadden. They said that

W. H. G. Kingston

they had themselves been scarcely a year before untaught savages, but that a large ship came to their shores, and that those in her treated them kindly, and that a missionary was sent who had taught them the new way; that they found it very good, and that their great wish was to act in accordance with the precepts of Christianity. The missionary, who had come from Raratonga, was living not far off, and would soon be with them. Mr Manners, on hearing this account, and calculating the position of the island, had little doubt that this was the island visited by the Ajax, the natives of which had at first given so hostile a reception to those who had landed on their shores, but had finally been won over by kindness. This opinion was confirmed when the missionary, a very intelligent Tahitian, arrived. He said that the people had welcomed him from the first, and that all of them, young and old, seemed anxious to learn the Truth.

Mr Manners was satisfied from all he saw and heard that a genuine change had taken place among the people. He found that, though tolerably industrious, and improving in that respect also, they did not produce as yet much more food than they required for their own support. He was therefore unwilling to remain longer among them than was necessary. All his efforts, however, to get the canoe repaired were useless, as some of her principal beams were broken, and it became necessary to pull her to pieces and to rebuild her. He hoped, however, that, before that could be done, the island would be visited by the missionary vessel, which would either carry him and his people off, or through which he might inform Captain Bertram where he was. In the meantime, that they might not be a burden to the inhabitants, he advised Marco to offer the services of his people to assist in cultivating the ground, while he and his seamen set to work to erect more comfortable huts than any which he had seen on the island. Marco did not refuse to labour with his hands, but he was also actively employed in assisting the missionary in preaching to and teaching the people. In this he was helped by several of his companions. Schools, both for adults and children, were also formed, and visible progress was made.

Three months fled rapidly by, when one day a native came running up to Mr Manners' hut, to tell him that a vessel was approaching the island. He at once went, accompanied by most of his men, to the highest spot in the neighbourhood, whence he could have a good look-out over the sea. His heart leaped for joy, for the ship, there could be little doubt of it, was the Ajax herself. The seamen one and all were agreed that she was their own ship. She hove to, a boat came on shore, and Mr Martin and his crew were cordially welcomed by their shipmates. The loss of the schooner, in consequence of her non-arrival, had been supposed probable, and the Ajax was now on a cruise to ascertain her fate, and to rescue any of the survivors of those who had been on board. After doing this, she was to return to Callao, where the admiral in the Pacific then was.

It is not necessary to describe the reception Mr Manners and his people met with on board their ship. Mr Martin was thankful to get back his son, and more so when he discovered the great change which had taken place in him. Ned was at once rated on the books of the Ajax as one of her crew. He had greatly improved since he had been discovered, and, with Ben constantly at his side, assisted also by Mr Manners, he continued to progress in Christian knowledge, as well as to improve in conduct and manners. Captain Bertram offered to receive Marco and his fellow-islanders on board. Two begged to remain where they were; the rest accepted his offer, Marco begging that he, with two others who had volunteered to accompany him, might be landed on the island on which Ned Hadden had so long resided. This Captain Bertram undertook to do, hoping that the appearance of a ship-of-war might awe the natives, and induce them to treat the missionaries with due respect. This plan was carried out, and Ned, who went on shore first, succeeded in extracting a promise from their chief that he would protect them. After landing the natives at their respective islands, the Ajax returned to Callao. There she remained till her term of service had expired, and she once more made sail for Old England. Amply was Ben Hadden repaid for all the dangers he had gone through when he was able to present his long-lost brother Ned to their widowed mother, not only rescued from the power of the savages, but from the dominion of sin and Satan.

And now there is not much more to tell about Ben Hadden. The experience he had had of a seafaring life confirmed his original desire to be a sailor; and the favour he had won, by his good conduct, in the regards of the captain and officers of the Ajax, was of great advantage to him, and led to his promotion in the service. When last we heard of him, Ben was what is called a warrant-officer, on board an admiral's ship—that admiral being his first patron and captain.

As long as his mother lived, Ben had the happiness of doing very much for her comfort, and also in assisting his older brother Ned in obtaining a good situation on shore; for he had had enough of the sea and savages, he said. So Mrs Hadden, though she remembered with a feeling of sadness the loss of her husband and other sons, yet felt and thankfully acknowledged that her God and Saviour had been very good to her in sparing those two—Ned and Ben; both of whom heartily adopted, and lived according to, their father's favourite motto:

"Do Right, whatever comes of it; And Trust in God."

ABOUT THE AUTHOR

William Henry Giles Kingston (1814 - 1880), writer of tales for boys, born in London, but spent much of his youth in Oporto, where his father was a merchant.

His first book, The Circassian Chief, appeared in 1844. His first book for boys, Peter the Whaler, was published in 1851, and had such success that he retired from business and devoted himself entirely to the production of this kind of literature, in which his popularity was deservedly great; and during 30 years he wrote upwards of 130 tales, including The Three Midshipmen (1862), The Three Lieutenants (1874), The Three Commanders (1875), The Three Admirals (1877), Digby Heathcote, etc.

He also conducted various papers, including The Colonist, and Colonial Magazine and East India Review. He was also interested in emigration, volunteering, and various philanthropic schemes. For services in negotiating a commercial treaty with Portugal he received a Portuguese knighthood, and for his literary labours a Government pension.

Choose from Thousands of 1stWorldLibrary Classics By

A. M. Barnard
Ada Leverson
Adolphus William Ward
Aesop
Agatha Christie
Alexander Aaronsohn
Alexander Kielland
Alexandre Dumas
Alfred Gatty
Alfred Ollivant
Alice Duer Miller
Alice Turner Curtis
Alice Dunbar
Allen Chapman
Alleyne Ireland
Ambrose Bierce
Amelia E. Barr
Amory H. Bradford
Andrew Lang
Andrew McFarland Davis
Andy Adams
Angela Brazil
Anna Alice Chapin
Anna Sewell
Annie Besant
Annie Hamilton Donnell
Annie Payson Call
Annie Roe Carr
Annonaymous
Anton Chekhov
Archibald Lee Fletcher
Arnold Bennett
Arthur C. Benson
Arthur Conan Doyle
Arthur M. Winfield
Arthur Ransome
Arthur Schnitzler
Arthur Train
Atticus
B.H. Baden-Powell
B. M. Bower
B. C. Chatterjee
Baroness Emmuska Orczy
Baroness Orczy
Basil King
Bayard Taylor
Ben Macomber
Bertha Muzzy Bower
Bjornstjerne Bjornson

Booth Tarkington
Boyd Cable
Bram Stoker
C. Collodi
C. E. Orr
C. M. Ingleby
Carolyn Wells
Catherine Parr Traill
Charles A. Eastman
Charles Amory Beach
Charles Dickens
Charles Dudley Warner
Charles Farrar Browne
Charles Ives
Charles Kingsley
Charles Klein
Charles Hanson Towne
Charles Lathrop Pack
Charles Romyn Dake
Charles Whibley
Charles Willing Beale
Charlotte M. Braeme
Charlotte M. Yonge
Charlotte Perkins Stetson
Clair W. Hayes
Clarence Day Jr.
Clarence E. Mulford
Clemence Housman
Confucius
Coningsby Dawson
Cornelis DeWitt Wilcox
Cyril Burleigh
D. H. Lawrence
Daniel Defoe
David Garnett
Dinah Craik
Don Carlos Janes
Donald Keyhoe
Dorothy Kilner
Dougan Clark
Douglas Fairbanks
E. Nesbit
E. P. Roe
E. Phillips Oppenheim
E. S. Brooks
Earl Barnes
Edgar Rice Burroughs
Edith Van Dyne
Edith Wharton

Edward Everett Hale
Edward J. O'Biren
Edward S. Ellis
Edwin L. Arnold
Eleanor Atkins
Eleanor Hallowell Abbott
Eliot Gregory
Elizabeth Gaskell
Elizabeth McCracken
Elizabeth Von Arnim
Ellem Key
Emerson Hough
Emilie F. Carlen
Emily Bronte
Emily Dickinson
Enid Bagnold
Enilor Macartney Lane
Erasmus W. Jones
Ernie Howard Pie
Ethel May Dell
Ethel Turner
Ethel Watts Mumford
Eugene Sue
Eugenie Foa
Eugene Wood
Eustace Hale Ball
Evelyn Everett-green
Everard Cotes
F. H. Cheley
F. J. Cross
F. Marion Crawford
Fannie E. Newberry
Federick Austin Ogg
Ferdinand Ossendowski
Fergus Hume
Florence A. Kilpatrick
Fremont B. Deering
Francis Bacon
Francis Darwin
Frances Hodgson Burnett
Frances Parkinson Keyes
Frank Gee Patchin
Frank Harris
Frank Jewett Mather
Frank L. Packard
Frank V. Webster
Frederic Stewart Isham
Frederick Trevor Hill
Frederick Winslow Taylor

Friedrich Kerst	Hayden Carruth	James Branch Cabell
Friedrich Nietzsche	Helent Hunt Jackson	James DeMille
Fyodor Dostoyevsky	Helen Nicolay	James Joyce
G.A. Henty	Hendrik Conscience	James Lane Allen
G.K. Chesterton	Hendy David Thoreau	James Lane Allen
Gabrielle E. Jackson	Henri Barbusse	James Oliver Curwood
Garrett P. Serviss	Henrik Ibsen	James Oppenheim
Gaston Leroux	Henry Adams	James Otis
George A. Warren	Henry Ford	James R. Driscoll
George Ade	Henry Frost	Jane Abbott
Geroge Bernard Shaw	Henry James	Jane Austen
George Cary Eggleston	Henry Jones Ford	Jane L. Stewart
George Durston	Henry Seton Merriman	Janet Aldridge
George Ebers	Henry W Longfellow	Jens Peter Jacobsen
George Eliot	Herbert A. Giles	Jerome K. Jerome
George Gissing	Herbert Carter	Jessie Graham Flower
George MacDonald	Herbert N. Casson	John Buchan
George Meredith	Herman Hesse	John Burroughs
George Orwell	Hildegard G. Frey	John Cournos
George Sylvester Viereck	Homer	John F. Kennedy
George Tucker	Honore De Balzac	John Gay
George W. Cable	Horace B. Day	John Glasworthy
George Wharton James	Horace Walpole	John Habberton
Gertrude Atherton	Horatio Alger Jr.	John Joy Bell
Gordon Casserly	Howard Pyle	John Kendrick Bangs
Grace E. King	Howard R. Garis	John Milton
Grace Gallatin	Hugh Lofting	John Philip Sousa
Grace Greenwood	Hugh Walpole	John Taintor Foote
Grant Allen	Humphry Ward	Jonas Lauritz Idemil Lie
Guillermo A. Sherwell	Ian Maclaren	Jonathan Swift
Gulielma Zollinger	Inez Haynes Gillmore	Joseph A. Altsheler
Gustav Flaubert	Irving Bacheller	Joseph Carey
H. A. Cody	Isabel Cecilia Williams	Joseph Conrad
H. B. Irving	Isabel Hornibrook	Joseph E. Badger Jr
H.C. Bailey	Israel Abrahams	Joseph Hergesheimer
H. G. Wells	Ivan Turgenev	Joseph Jacobs
H. H. Munro	J.G.Austin	Jules Vernes
H. Irving Hancock	J. Henri Fabre	Julian Hawthrone
H. R. Naylor	J. M. Barrie	Julie A Lippmann
H. Rider Haggard	J. M. Walsh	Justin Huntly McCarthy
H. W. C. Davis	J. Macdonald Oxley	Kakuzo Okakura
Haldeman Julius	J. R. Miller	Karle Wilson Baker
Hall Caine	J. S. Fletcher	Kate Chopin
Hamilton Wright Mabie	J. S. Knowles	Kenneth Grahame
Hans Christian Andersen	J. Storer Clouston	Kenneth McGaffey
Harold Avery	J. W. Duffield	Kate Langley Bosher
Harold McGrath	Jack London	Kate Langley Bosher
Harriet Beecher Stowe	Jacob Abbott	Katherine Cecil Thurston
Harry Castlemon	James Allen	Katherine Stokes
Harry Coghill	James Andrews	L. A. Abbot
Harry Houidini	James Baldwin	L. T. Meade

L. Frank Baum
Latta Griswold
Laura Dent Crane
Laura Lee Hope
Laurence Housman
Lawrence Beasley
Leo Tolstoy
Leonid Andreyev
Lewis Carroll
Lewis Sperry Chafer
Lilian Bell
Lloyd Osbourne
Louis Hughes
Louis Joseph Vance
Louis Tracy
Louisa May Alcott
Lucy Fitch Perkins
Lucy Maud Montgomery
Luther Benson
Lydia Miller Middleton
Lyndon Orr
M. Corvus
M. H. Adams
Margaret E. Sangster
Margret Howth
Margaret Vandercook
Margaret W. Hungerford
Margret Penrose
Maria Edgeworth
Maria Thompson Daviess
Mariano Azuela
Marion Polk Angellotti
Mark Overton
Mark Twain
Mary Austin
Mary Catherine Crowley
Mary Cole
Mary Hastings Bradley
Mary Roberts Rinehart
Mary Rowlandson
M. Wollstonecraft Shelley
Maud Lindsay
Max Beerbohm
Myra Kelly
Nathaniel Hawthrone
Nicolo Machiavelli
O. F. Walton
Oscar Wilde
Owen Johnson
P.G. Wodehouse
Paul and Mabel Thorne

Paul G. Tomlinson
Paul Severing
Percy Brebner
Percy Keese Fitzhugh
Peter B. Kyne
Plato
Quincy Allen
R. Derby Holmes
R. L. Stevenson
R. S. Ball
Rabindranath Tagore
Rahul Alvares
Ralph Bonehill
Ralph Henry Barbour
Ralph Victor
Ralph Waldo Emmerson
Rene Descartes
Ray Cummings
Rex Beach
Rex E. Beach
Richard Harding Davis
Richard Jefferies
Richard Le Gallienne
Robert Barr
Robert Frost
Robert Gordon Anderson
Robert L. Drake
Robert Lansing
Robert Lynd
Robert Michael Ballantyne
Robert W. Chambers
Rosa Nouchette Carey
Rudyard Kipling
Saint Augustine
Samuel B. Allison
Samuel Hopkins Adams
Sarah Bernhardt
Sarah C. Hallowell
Selma Lagerlof
Sherwood Anderson
Sigmund Freud
Standish O'Grady
Stanley Weyman
Stella Benson
Stella M. Francis
Stephen Crane
Stewart Edward White
Stijn Streuvels
Swami Abhedananda
Swami Parmananda
T. S. Ackland

T. S. Arthur
The Princess Der Ling
Thomas A. Janvier
Thomas A Kempis
Thomas Anderton
Thomas Bailey Aldrich
Thomas Bulfinch
Thomas De Quincey
Thomas Dixon
Thomas H. Huxley
Thomas Hardy
Thomas More
Thornton W. Burgess
U. S. Grant
Upton Sinclair
Valentine Williams
Various Authors
Vaughan Kester
Victor Appleton
Victor G. Durham
Victoria Cross
Virginia Woolf
Wadsworth Camp
Walter Camp
Walter Scott
Washington Irving
Wilbur Lawton
Wilkie Collins
Willa Cather
Willard F. Baker
William Dean Howells
William le Queux
W. Makepeace Thackeray
William W. Walter
William Shakespeare
Winston Churchill
Yei Theodora Ozaki
Yogi Ramacharaka
Young E. Allison
Zane Grey